Essentials of Special E

In this succinct yet comprehensive text, authors Lawless Frank and Richards guide readers through the essential basics that every educator needs to know about special education, covering everything from law to application.

Streamlined and accessible chapters address legal knowledge – Section 504, IDEA, ESSA, and FERPA – assessment and identification, RTI, categories of disability, IEPs, accommodations, co-teaching, and instructional considerations.

Designed to give new educators a focused introduction to critical concepts and terminology, this book also features supplemental online resources including an Instructor's Manual, quizzes, and more.

Catherine Lawless Frank is an Assistant Professor in the School of Education and Health Sciences at the University of Dayton, USA.

Stephen B. Richards is Associate Professor of Teacher Education in the College of Education and Human Performance at West Liberty University, USA.

Essentials of Special Education

What Educators Need to Know

Catherine Lawless Frank and
Stephen B. Richards

Routledge
Taylor & Francis Group

NEW YORK AND LONDON

First published 2021
by Routledge
52 Vanderbilt Avenue, New York, NY 10017

and by Routledge
2 Park Square, Milton Park, Abingdon, Oxon OX14 4RN

Routledge is an imprint of the Taylor & Francis Group, an informa business

© 2021 Taylor & Francis

Library of Congress Cataloging-in-Publication Data
A catalog record for this title has been requested

ISBN: 978-0-367-36711-4 (hbk)
ISBN: 978-0-367-41656-0 (pbk)
ISBN: 978-0-367-81553-0 (ebk)

Typeset in Goudy
by Taylor & Francis Books

Contents

Figures

Tables

1 Legal Aspects of Special Education

Stephen B. Richards and Sarah Schimmel

Objectives: After reading this chapter, you should be able to:

1 Identify and explain the rights and responsibilities of parents
2 Identify and explain the provisions of Section 504
3 Identify and explain the provisions of the Individuals with Disabilities Education Improvement Act
4 Identify and explain the provisions of the Every Student Succeeds Act
5 Identify and explain the provisions of the Family Educational Rights and Privacy Act.

General education teachers are often the bridge to special education for a student and their family. Typically, they are the first to notice and report academic or behavioral concerns and advocate for additional supports and services. Their primary responsibilities involve teaching and monitoring students' progress, including students with disabilities and other diverse learning needs. The vast majority of students with disabilities spend most, if not all, of their school day alongside their general education peers and are educated by general education teachers. In almost every aspect of special education, from referral to determining eligibility to writing and implementing Individualized Education Programs, general education teachers are vital partners.

The initial relationships that schools develop with students, parents, and families (in this text, the terms parent and families are used as general terms for the primary caregiver of a child) typically start with a general education teacher. This relationship can help parents navigate the complexities of Multi-Tiered Systems of Support (MTSS) and special education. MTSS, which includes Response to Intervention (RTI), provides increasing intervention levels to students based on needs with the possible referral and implementation of special education services if warranted. General education teachers often have the closest relationships with families in the initial phases of special education. They may be called upon to explain MTSS, the referral and eligibility for special education process, answer questions, and reassure parents of their child's rights. They are the link between parents and the school personnel involved in the initial referral and determining the eligibility of a child for special education.

In this text, we will discuss some of the key aspects of special education, focusing on those that are most critical to general education teachers. Chapter 2 will examine MTSS and the general education teachers' role in all levels or tiers of the process, including providing data-driven instruction to an inclusive classroom, small groups, and possibly intensive individualized instruction. In each tier, these teachers are also responsible for monitoring student progress towards Individualized Education Program (IEP) goals or for documentation to advocate for additional supports and possibly special education services.

General education teachers play a critical role in collecting the necessary data (see Chapter 3 for more information about the eligibility process) to determine whether a student is eligible for:

1 accommodations in the general education classrooms,
2 special education and related services, or
3 remaining in general education with no specific services required.

In each of those three scenarios, the general education teacher's collaborative role is essential to ensure the student's timely and impartial evaluation. These evaluations typically begin with a referral from a general education teacher.

To determine eligibility and provide instruction, general education teachers need to be aware of the 13 special education disabilities categories (see Chapter 4 for more information on the characteristics of each disability). Each disability's criteria provides a generalized characteristic of its impact on the student's ability to learn and participate in school. General education teachers play a critical role in looking beyond these disability traits to acknowledge the student's unique characteristics, strengths, and needs.

Each student with a disability has their own Individualized Education Program (IEP). The IEP documents their annual goals and the supports and services to help them achieve those goals (IEPs are discussed in more detail in Chapter 5). While the special education teacher typically writes the IEP, the general education teacher collaborates to formulate the appropriate goals, provide instruction, administer accommodations and modifications, and monitor the student's progress. They are essential members of the student's IEP team.

The components of effective teaching are the same for all students, including those with disabilities and other diverse learning needs. Instructional pedagogies such as direct instruction, sheltered instruction, and Universal Design for Learning incorporate the supports that facilitate learning. At times, students with disabilities are provided accommodations and modifications that are embedded into these pedagogies and documented on their IEPs or 504 Plans. Determining and implementing the appropriate accommodations and modifications is a collaborative team effort involving both general and special education as well as parents and school administrators (for more information on pedagogies, accommodations, 504 Plans, and modifications see Chapter 6).

The responsibilities for providing special education services do not occur in isolation. Teachers, administrators, aides, and related services personnel are also involved in instruction and addressing student progress. At times, this collaborative process may require co-teaching, in which the general education teacher shares the planning, teaching, and assessment of students with another professional. In co-teaching, the teachers form a partnership and share responsibility, students, and the classroom to meet the needs of all students better. More information on collaboration and co-teaching can be found in Chapter 7.

Educating a student involves more than merely providing academic content. Learning is a complex process that often requires additional instructional considerations. Chapter 8 will discuss some of these overarching educational concerns, such as executive functioning, learning strategies, metacognition, and social skills, that facilitate the learning process.

We will begin this text with a chapter on the legal basis and foundation of special education. Laws including the Individuals with Disabilities Education Improvement Act and Section 504 of the Rehabilitation Act provide the framework and provisions for special education services and accommodations. The Every Student Succeeds Act and Family Education Rights and Privacy Act apply to all students and set parameters for state- and district-wide assessment and privacy issues. These laws guide special education processes and provide protection for students with disabilities and their parents.

Parent Rights and Responsibilities

Once a decision is made to conduct a multi-factor team evaluation (MFE), a multi-disciplinary evaluation team (MDET) is formed. This team conducts the evaluation to determine whether a student is eligible for special education and related services. At this time, several "due process" mechanisms are required. Among the first is for the school district to ensure:

1   parents are fully informed, in a written notification and orally as needed, as to what the district is proposing to do; the district must document its efforts to inform parents;
2   this written and oral notification is in the parents' native language, and an interpreter is available as needed for any meeting or communications.

These requirements apply to all communications and meetings concerning the evaluation, placement, and services provided to the student. Due process requirements apply while the student is under consideration even if a student is not ultimately identified for special education.

Once determined that an MFE is needed:

1   the district must obtain the informed consent of the parents before personnel may conduct any evaluations;
2   parents are members of the evaluation team and may contribute their information, thoughts, and experiences to the other members for consideration in the MFE;
3   parents may obtain their own independent evaluation (from professionals such as an educational psychologist not associated with the school) and have those results considered in the MFE;
4   parents must be informed of the results of the MFE within 60 days of giving consent;
5   if their child is eligible for special education and related services, the district must develop an IEP within 30 days, with the parents as members of the IEP team as well; and
6   the district must again obtain informed consent from parents to implement the IEP; the first consent mentioned is *only* for conducting the MFE; this second consent is to approve the placement of the student in special education and implementation of the student's IEP (West Virginia Department of Education, Policy 2419 retrieved from www.wvde.us, 05/2020).

General education teachers are involved in the MFE, providing information and data related to the student's classroom performance. They are members of the IEP team if there is even the *possibility* the student will be included in general education (which is the vast majority of students on IEPs). They may also be involved in implementing services/accommodations included in the IEP, teaching goals, and progress monitoring. This can sound daunting, but special education, and possibly related services staff will be collaborative partners in the processes. There is a special education teacher or administrator assigned as the individual responsible for overseeing the monitoring and implementation of the IEP.

Case Study 1.1

You are a special education teacher working with a team of 3rd grade general education teachers. One teacher, Ms. Carlie, has a student Katie who is falling further and further behind her peers in reading, writing, and spelling. Katie has been through the multi-tier system of supports required and the interventions have not increased her progress sufficiently. Another teacher, Ms. Farnbach, thinks Katie should be referred for evaluation for special education. A third teacher, Ms. Harper, is on board with the other team members' thoughts.

Ms. Carlie thinks the evaluation should start immediately – the next day. The school psychologist is scheduled to be in the building to assess another student and the psychologist already knows Katie. Ms. Carlie says "I could ask her to do a couple of assessments – an achievement test and IQ test – that might tell us more." Ms. Farnbach agrees the test results might help, but she is concerned about whether they should go ahead without at least talking to Katie's parents. Ms. Carlie and Ms. Harper say they know Katie's parents very well and the parents are aware Katie has academic issues. Ms. Carlie and Ms. Harper insist they should begin tomorrow; one of them says, "I guarantee Katie's parents will be on board with this."

As the special education teacher:

1 What would be your input regarding beginning the evaluation the next day?
2 What step(s) would you suggest be taken as soon as possible?

General education teachers can help keep parents informed, reassure them their student is being treated fairly, and that the IEP is in the student's best interest. Of course, any IEP member who dissents from any portion of an IEP may voice their disagreement in writing and at the IEP meeting. However, school personnel dissent will not prevent the implementation of an IEP so long as the parents have consented. Once the individual at the IEP meeting who is the local education agency (typically the school district) representative signs off on the IEP, *all* district personnel are required to comply with the provisions of the IEP, regardless of whether they dissent (Richards, Frank, Sableski, & Arnold, 2019).

If a student has reached the "age of majority" (18 years in most states), the student can take the parents' place in terms of consent and participation as they are legally an adult. Even if a student does not exercise these rights and the parents remain "in charge," inviting the student to participate in the IEP process is encouraged by many experts.

More details concerning the MFE and IEP process are presented in Chapters 3 and 5, respectively. The IEP, in particular, is the document most impacting K-12 students in special education and both their general and special education teachers. Not all students who struggle in the general education classroom qualify for special education under the requirements of the Individuals with Disabilities Education Improvement Act (IDEA). The MFE may determine that a student does not meet the criteria for special education. Students with mild attentional difficulties, difficulties in taking tests or assessments when distractions are present, and similar conditions may not warrant special education but may merit specific accommodations. When this situation arises, a student may qualify for a 504 Plan under Section 504 of the Rehabilitation Act.

Comprehension Check

1 What are parents' rights involving permission for the evaluation for and implementation of special education for their child?

2 What must the school district do if a child's parents are immigrants and their first language is not English?

3 When can a student legally "take charge" of their education and give or withhold consent without their parents?

Section 504 of the Rehabilitation Act

The Rehabilitation Act is a federal law passed in 1973 that included Section 504. It has many implications for people with disabilities both in and out of school. In essence, this provision of the act states that no individual by reason of disability alone may be excluded from any program receiving federal assistance. Specifically, the law says:

> No otherwise qualified individual with a disability in the United States ... shall, solely by reason of her or his disability, be excluded from the participation in, be denied the benefits of, or be subjected to discrimination under any program or activity receiving federal financial assistance (29 U.S.C. 794).

As amended in 1974, Section 111, Pub L. 93–516, 88 Stat. 1619 (Dec. 7, 1974), *Individuals with Disabilities* are:

> Any person who (a) has a physical or mental impairment which substantially limits one or more of such person's major life activities, (b) has a record of such an impairment, or (c) is regarded as having such an impairment.

Major life activities include caring for oneself, walking, seeing, hearing, speaking, breathing, working, performing manual tasks, and learning.

Of course, all public schools and universities receive federal funding, but so do many private universities through grants, federal student financial aid, and other sources. Section 504 provides accommodations for students in K-12 and higher education settings through a 504 plan. Section 504 does not qualify a student for special education. Instead, it provides means for "leveling the playing field" for students with conditions that qualify under Section 504. However, a school district may offer special education services as there is *no prohibition* against it.

Qualifying for a 504 plan is generally less involved than qualifying for an IEP. Section 504 only requires that an individual has a condition that impairs a major life activity for a substantial period of time (for instance, attention deficit disorder or asthma) (Office for Civil Rights, The civil rights of students with hidden disabilities under Section 504 of the Rehabilitation Act of 1973, retrieved from www.ed.gov, 10/2018). Examples of accommodations for students on a 504 plan (sometimes referred to as an accommodations plan) include preferential seating, extended time on tests, and distraction-free environment for tests. These accommodations are provided in the general education environment and do not require placement in a special education classroom.

Comprehension Check

1   How does Section 504 help a child in school?
2   Why would private universities have to abide by Section 504 rules?
3   Do students on 504 plans always receive special education services? Why or why not?

Individuals with Disabilities Education Improvement Act (IDEA)

The IDEA was initially signed into law in 1975 and has been reauthorized several times since then. The most recent reauthorization was in 2004. The most recent revisions to special education processes and requirements were in 2015 in the Every Student Succeeds Act (discussed later in the chapter). Since 1975, the major provisions of IDEA have remained, although some have been added in subsequent reauthorizations. These six provisions include the rights of eligible students to:

1   a free, appropriate public education,
2   nondiscriminatory evaluation,
3   individualized education program,
4   education in the least restrictive environment,
5   due process procedures to ensure equitable treatment and opportunity, and
6   parent participation in all phases of the special education processes (Smiley, Richards, & Taylor, 2019).

In 1986, services for infants, toddlers, and preschoolers were included in the law. In 1997, a provision for students on IEPs to participate in statewide assessments (achievement testing, for example) or an alternate assessment as appropriate was included. Part C of IDEA includes provisions for early intervention for children from birth to three years of age. At age three, children transition from Part C to Part B, which provides services for students from ages three to 21 years. A plan for transitioning from Part C (birth to three years) to Part B (three to 21 years) and from high school to adult living is also now required. While these amendments to IDEA have strengthened the protections for students with disabilities, the six main provisions are the fundamental rights under the law from its origin to the present. The following sections are summarized from the U.S. Department of Education, IDEA statute and regulations, retrieved from www.sites.ed.gov, 06/2020 (Richards et al., 2016; Smiley et al., 2019).

Free, Appropriate Public Education (FAPE)

In 1972, The Pennsylvania Association for Retarded Children (PARC) (currently known as The Arc – omitting the term "retarded" from the national organization's title) was involved in a lawsuit with the Commonwealth of Pennsylvania. The issue was whether children with severe developmental disabilities that needed supports and modifications could be legally excluded from school. The court sided with PARC and set the legal precedent for the FAPE requirement of IDEA in 1975. Other court cases (e.g., *Mills v. Board of Education of District of Columbia*, 1972) also contributed to the conception of FAPE.

FAPE may initially appear as a rather straightforward requirement, but it does have various ramifications for school districts and families of students with disabilities. First, the "Free" in FAPE means that the child's education is without costs to parents. The education of any student with a disability can include expenses for the school district that are in excess of the cost of educating a student without disabilities. Expenses can range from few to considerable costs but is free to parents regardless of the excess costs. The "appropriate" may be less clear cut. Numerous legal actions have occurred over the years when families and school districts have disagreed about what constitutes an appropriate education for a child.

For example, a parent might request a child with autism be provided with Applied Behavior Analysis therapy that can have a considerable cost if provided through a community agency. The school district may assert that they have trained teachers to work with children with autism, and the costly out of school program is not necessary to provide an appropriate education. Overall, legal actions have resulted in a recognition that "appropriate" education does not translate to the best possible education. The education and services must be sufficient for the student to meet their educational needs as established on the Individualized Education Program. Nevertheless, there are instances where the courts have ruled in favor of parents and in favor of school districts depending on the particular circumstances and arguments (e.g., review the case of *Hendrick Hudson Central School District v. Rowley*, 1982 and *Endrew F. v. Douglas County School District*, 2017).

The term "public" establishes that students with disabilities should attend the same public schools they might if they had no disabilities. Finally, the term "education" can be broadly construed to include the general education curriculum and classes, accommodations within general education, modifications to the general education program, special education only, and even residential placements if required. This is often referred to as a continuum of services as depicted in Figure 1.1 (adapted from West Virginia Department of Education, Hand in hand guidance for West Virginia families, retrieved from www.wvde.us, 06/2020).

General educators are involved in the delivery of FAPE to the vast majority of students in special education, especially since typically 50% or more of each school day is spent in general education classes using a general education curriculum for most students with disabilities.

Nondiscriminatory Evaluation

In 1972, a class-action lawsuit in California (*Larry P. v. Riles*) questioned the placement of African American students in classes for students with mild intellectual disabilities based mainly on intelligence testing. The plaintiffs argued that such practices were discriminatory toward African American students. Similar lawsuits have addressed the

---

(More Restrictive) Residential School (The Fewest Students Served)
Student receives special education and related services from specially trained staff in a residential facility in which children receive care or services 24 hours a day.

Separate School
Student receives special education and related services under the direction of a specially trained staff in a specially designed facility (day program).

Separate Classroom
Student attends a special class for most or all of the school day and receives special education and related services under the direction of a special education teacher.

Resource Room
Student is in the regular classroom for the majority of the school day but goes to the special education resource room for specialized instruction for part of each school day.

Regular Classroom with Supplementary Instruction and Services
Student receives a prescribed program under the direction of the regular classroom teacher and also receives instruction and related services within the regular classroom from the special educator and/or a paraeducator.

Regular Classroom with Consultation
Student receives a prescribed program under the direction of the regular classroom teacher, who is supported by ongoing consultation from the special educator(s).

(Least Restrictive) Regular Classroom
Student receives a prescribed program under the direction of the regular classroom teacher.

Figure 1.1 Continuum of Services

evaluation of students whose first language was not English (*Diana v. CA Board of Education*, 1970). These students were placed in special education based on assessments conducted without regard to the students' primary language and possible limited English proficiency. In a nutshell, it could be said states and school districts were using discriminatory practices to identify students for special education. Therefore, the processes used to determine eligibility and placement of students in special education must be free of any bias that places a student at a disadvantage. It should be evident through the MFE and parental consent that special education placement and delivery is in the student's best interests.

IDEA specifies that parental consent to evaluate a student is required prior to the MFE. Assessments must be valid and reliable (assessments that yield results that should not radically change in a short period of time and are useful for what the assessment is designed for). Assessments should be individually administered and not group tests only. Assessments must be given in the student's native language. As previously noted, assessments must not be discriminatory toward the student (e.g., requiring a student with a known visual impairment to perform written tasks that are not modified for the student's visual issues). Parents also have the right to have their own evaluation done and have the school district consider those evaluation results. The MDET that conducts the MFE must obtain data from multiple sources and involve multiple people on the team, including parents and general and special educators. A school administrator is typically a member as is a school psychologist or other professional knowledgeable about the assessments used. Other professionals such as a speech and language pathologist, adaptive physical education teacher, a behavior specialist, or an occupational therapist may also be included based on need. Once the multi-disciplinary evaluation is conducted, a team including the parents determines whether the student meets the state criteria for one of the IDEA disability categories (discussed in detail in Chapter 4).

For example, for determining whether a student has an intellectual disability, the team must establish, through classroom performance and assessments, that the student has significantly sub-average intellectual functioning and deficits in adaptive skills and concepts (e.g., telling time, self-care, money skills). These issues must have emerged between birth and 18 years of age, adversely affect educational performance, and require special education services. The process from obtaining parental consent for a multi-disciplinary evaluation to actually determining eligibility should occur within 60 days.

Individualized Education Program (IEP)

Once eligibility is established under one of the IDEA disability categories, a team is formed, including the parents, to develop an IEP. It is important to note that parental consent for the multi-disciplinary evaluation is *not* also consent for the implementation of special education and related services. Therefore, while an IEP may be written, it cannot be *implemented* without again receiving parental consent. In other words, a parent could give consent for the MFE, special education eligibility determined under a disability category, and an IEP written. However, the parents still have the right to refuse the implementation of special education and related services.

The IEP includes several components that the team must address. These are discussed in greater detail in Chapter 5. In general, though, an IEP consists of the student's annual learning goals and the services required to achieve those goals. IEPs are applicable for students served under Part B (ages three to 21 years) of IDEA.

Children from birth to three years of age are served under Part C of IDEA, and provided services through an Individualized Family Service Plan (IFSP) rather than an IEP. These plans are similar, but the IFSP is geared towards the family unit while the IEP focuses on the individual child. Services on an IFSP could involve parent training, social services, and delivery of educational services in the home rather than in a school setting.

The team must update both IEPs and IFSPs at least annually. Students on IEPs must also be reevaluated by the multi-disciplinary evaluation team every three years. As mentioned previously, IFSPs must include transition plans for the change from Part C to Part B services. IEPs must include transition plans for students exiting from school services. This transition plan must begin no later than 16 years of age.

Least Restrictive Environment (LRE)

A provision of IDEA is that students on IEPs be educated with their non-disabled peers to the maximum extent *appropriate*. Note this provision does not specify to the maximum extent *possible*. There is an assumption that students on IEPs should be educated with their nondisabled chronological-age peers in the school they would attend if they did not have a disability. This placement is the least restrictive environment (LRE) for most students with disabilities. Based on the IEP annual goals and services needed, a student might spend time during the school day in a resource or "pull out" room (a part-time special education class) or even a separate special education classroom all day. Refer back to Figure 1.1 for the continuum of services and placements. The key to LRE is the student being educated in the environments that are most conducive to achieving the IEP goals and allows the student to continue to be engaged with peers. It is essential to note that the IEP team's LRE decision is individualized and based on the student's needs. The LRE is *not* determined by the disability category nor soley by the special education services needed.

A student on an IEP should not attend a special class for students with intellectual disabilities simply because that is their disability.

Similarly, a student who is deaf would not necessarily be educated only by teachers certified in teaching students who are deaf or hard of hearing. Special education and related services can be delivered in general education environments. These are sometimes referred to as "push-in" services as they are delivered in the general education classrooms. A determination of a disability does not require a special education class placement, although part-time placement in a resource or pull out room is not unusual. Figure 1.2 includes data regarding in what environments students with disabilities receive their education and to what extent.

Due Process Procedures

Various due process procedures must be followed in identifying a student for special education and implementing services. These procedures are designed to ensure fair treatment and protection of due process rights. For example, parental consent for conducting an MFE and consent to implement an IEP are components of due process procedures. The policies and procedures manual for implementing all aspects of special education, available in each state, is typically a lengthy document with guidelines for schools and educators, all of which could be considered due process procedures. These procedures are designed to avoid discrimination, provide equal and appropriate educational opportunities, and protect student and parent rights. These include nondiscriminatory evaluation, parental participation, annual reviews of IEPs, and so on.

However, in everyday use, educators may use the term "due process procedures" to describe the steps that occur when a family and school district are at odds over an issue related to the identification of a student or the provision of services. As mentioned earlier, what constitutes an "appropriate" education or which environment is the "least restrictive" may be areas of disagreement. Even the implementation of the policies and procedures for ensuring due process may be contested at times (e.g., were parents notified in writing promptly of the school district's

---

As of Fall, 2017:

63% of students spent 80% or more of their school time in general education classes

18% of students spent between 40–79% of their school time in general education classes

13% of students spent less than 40% of their school time in general education classes

6% of students were served in other placements

Figure 1.2 Percentage of Students with Disabilities Ages 6–21 Years and Placements Source: U.S. Department of Education, Children and Youth with Disabilities, Chapter 1: Preprimary, primary, and secondary education. Retrieved from www.nces.ed.gov, 06/2020.

intentions in providing special education to a child). In such situations, IDEA outlines steps for school districts and families to follow to resolve differences. These due process procedures are designed to identify what is in the student's best interests, that neither party has violated rights and responsibilities, and that both the school districts and families receive unbiased mediation of differences. However, sometimes lawsuits are filed and ruled on when the two parties cannot come to some resolution under IDEA procedures.

General and special educators need to recognize they could be involved in due process proceedings. These proceedings can prove rather costly to both parties as a result of legal fees and other costs. Typically, everyone's interest is to resolve the issues without actually going to court. General and special educators *must* abide by the requirements for services included in the IEP regardless of whether one might personally agree or disagree with the IEP provisions. For example, if an IEP specifies a student should receive extended time for tests and assignments, a general or special education teacher must comply with those accommodations even if the educator does not believe the student should receive the accommodations.

Parental Participation

As mentioned previously, parents are to be involved in every aspect of their child's identification for and delivery of special education services. For example, parents must be given prior written notice of any meetings related to their child's education. Parents and their student have the right to give and refuse consent. Parents must receive both written and oral communication in their native language. Parents have the right to redress grievances through due process procedures.

The key here is that IDEA places parents in a position to provide input and substantially control the education their child receives. IDEA mandates that parents must be informed of and allowed to participate in all decision making, no matter their degree of perceived interest or involvement. State departments of education typically provide written manuals for parents outlining the special education and due processes in accessible and understandable language for families. School districts must ensure parents know and understand their rights and responsibilities. Finally, states typically provide taxpayer-funded parents' rights advocates who may work with the family to ensure their rights are protected (e.g., by attending an IEP meeting with parents).

Overall, IDEA is one of the more critical laws concerning public education.

It affects every public school and every educator. IDEA is regulated by the federal and state governments to ensure compliance with its provisions. General and special educators are wise to be apprised of what is required of them under state and federal laws.

Comprehension Check

1   What do the terms "free" and "appropriate" mean in FAPE?
2   What is an IEP?
3   What are due process procedures, and why do they exist in IDEA?

Every Student Succeeds Act

The Every Student Succeeds Act (ESSA) was passed in 2015 and replaced the No Child Left Behind Act (NCLB) passed in 2004. ESSA is not explicitly directed toward students with disabilities but instead all students and public schools. ESSA rolled back provisions of NCLB, but the impact on special education was limited. States must still include students on IEPs in statewide assessments. However, ESSA limits the number on alternate assessment (versus traditional academic progress assessments) to 1% of all students or approximately 10% of students in special education. In statewide assessments, schools must still identify subgroups of students, including those with disabilities, who are low performing and then develop evidence-based plans to assist in improving the performance of these groups. Districts must monitor progress using those plans and intervene if no improvement occurs. States and districts must also develop comprehensive improvement plans for schools with chronic low performing subgroups (Klein, The Every Student Succeeds Act: An ESSA Overview, retrieved 10/2018).

The requirements from NCLB for 95% participation in statewide testing is still in force, as well as allowances for accommodations for students with disabilities. Finally, ESSA has made some funding changes that may allow states to consolidate monies to better serve students with special needs and low-income students (Klein, The Every Student Succeeds Act: An ESSA Overview, retrieved 10/2018).

Comprehension Check

1   What law did ESSA replace, and discuss one way in which ESSA affects education?
2   Are students with disabilities still required to take state assessments of achievement (or measures of academic progress/proficiency)?
3   What percentage of students typically are allowed to participate in alternate assessments?

Family Education Rights and Privacy Act

The Family Education Rights and Privacy Act (FERPA) was passed in 1974 and provides protections for students (who have reached the age of majority) and parents in the area of school records and reports, regardless of whether a student has a disability. It is sometimes referred to as the Buckley Amendment. These protections include:

1   the right to review and inspect the student's school records;
2   the right to request corrections in school records if considered inaccurate or misleading and due process procedures if parents/student and the school disagrees; and
3   the right of consent for the school to release educational information, although there are various exceptions (e.g., school personnel who need to review the records, judicial orders, health and safety emergencies, among other exceptions).

Schools may publish general information such as name, address, phone number, and other directory information, but parents (or students age 18 or older) must be informed and allowed to request that such information not be published. Annually, schools must also notify parents/student of their rights under FERPA (U.S. Department of Education, Family Educational Rights and Privacy Act, retrieved from www.ed. gov, 02/2020). For all teachers, FERPA can be thought of in the simplest terms as a confidentiality law. Teachers *must* be careful not to share information about a student's education to others who do not have a "need to know." A teacher who shares information about a student with friends, relatives, or other parties who are not involved in the student's education runs the risks of both legal issues and the loss of their teaching position.

Case Study 1.2

You are out on Friday evening with two teachers who work in the same building as you (K-2 grades) and a third teacher who works in the grades 3–4 building next door. You are all going to a restaurant to eat. You are the designated driver so the others are also sharing wine before and during dinner. You go to talk to another friend at another table and when you return you hear the following conversation in progress.

"Well, let me tell you about MY 1st grader, Miguel. He has been such a challenge with his behavior, but then, yesterday I read something awful in his permanent school record that had a psychologist's report in it. When Miguel was 4 years old, an uncle of his was accused and convicted of sexually molesting Miguel and his brother. Miguel saw a counselor for sexually abused children for over a year. I wonder if all that might not be what's affecting his behavior?"

The other two colleagues remark, "How awful – poor Miguel!" and "Was it his mother's or father's brother – do you know? His parents are divorced now I hear and maybe this had something to do with that."

1   What if any issues could arise if someone heard this conversation at the next table whose grandchild attends the same school as Miguel and the grandchild talks about how "bad" Miguel is?
2   If you could say something as soon as the conversation begins, what would you tell your colleagues?

In this chapter, we have provided basic information about laws concerning the provision of educational services to students with disabilities, as well as students without disabilities. Special education teachers will need more detailed knowledge, particularly regarding IDEA. General education teachers should be familiar with the basic provisions of all these laws. A final reminder is that students who have reached the age of majority (18–21 years depending on the state) can exercise their rights under these laws if they so choose.

Comprehension Check

1   What does the acronym FERPA stand for?
2   What rights do parents and students have under FERPA?
3   What should teachers know about the confidentiality of school records?

References

Klein, A. The Every Student Succeeds Act: An ESSA Overview. *Education Week.* Retrieved from www.edweek.org, 10/2018.

Office for Civil Rights. The civil rights of students with hidden disabilities under Section 504 of the Rehabilitation Act of 1973. Retrieved from www.ed.gov, 10/2018.

Richards, S. B., Frank, C. L., Sableski, M. K., & Arnold, J. M., (2019). *Collaboration among professionals, students, families, and communities.* New York, NY: Routledge.

Smiley, L. R., Richards, S. B., & Taylor, R. L. (2019). *Exceptional students: Preparing teachers for the 21st Century* (3rd ed.). Columbus, OH: McGraw-Hill.

U.S. Department of Education. Family Educational Rights and Privacy Act (FERPA). Retrieved from www.ed.gov, 02/2020.

U.S. Department of Education. IDEA statute and regulations. Retrieved from www.sites.ed.gov, 06/2020.

West Virginia Department of Education (2020). Hand in hand guidance for West Virginia families. Retrieved from www.wvde.us, 05/2020.

West Virginia Department of Education (2017). *Regulations for the education of students with exceptionalities (with revisions).* Retrieved from www.wvde.us, 05/2020.

2 Multi-Tiered Systems of Support

Catherine Lawless Frank

Objectives: After reading this chapter, students will be able to:

1   Summarize the purpose and framework of Response to Intervention
2   Identify the different components of each tier in Response to Intervention
3   Describe the ongoing cycle of assessment, analysis, decision making, and instruction that forms the basis of Response to Intervention and effective teaching.

Overview of Multi-Tiered Systems of Support

Multi-Tiered Systems of Support (MTSS) such as Response to Intervention (RTI) provide students with the necessary instruction and interventions to make adequate academic and behavioral gains. This framework offers increasing levels of support for students who struggle through a tiered approach. Tier 1, or the basis of this approach, is data-driven instruction provided by a qualified teacher in a general education classroom using a valid curriculum. Tier 1 includes all students and meets the majority of the students' academic and behavioral needs. Ongoing assessments in critical academic areas are used to ensure students make adequate progress and identify those who are struggling. When the data indicates a student needs additional support, then supplementary services or interventions may be provided in Tier 2. Tier 2 services attempt to remediate areas of concern through focused instruction and help prevent inappropriate referrals to special education. Those students who continue to struggle after Tier 2 support may qualify for more intensive interventions in Tier 3 or special education. Throughout each tier, assessment results guide instruction, and increasing levels of support are provided based on the intensity of a student's individual needs.

Critical to any MTSS is data-driven instruction or the use of assessment data to inform subsequent instruction. This assessment process begins with an initial screening, typically referred to as universal screening, given to all students at the beginning of the school year to identify strengths and areas of concern. Instruction is then provided and guided, in part, by the assessment results. Students are reassessed on an ongoing basis to ensure that they are making sufficient gains. This continuing assessment data allows schools to intervene or adjust instruction accordingly to remediate and avoid further academic or behavioral concerns.

For example, Eliza was given an initial assessment or universal screening at the beginning of the school year in math, reading fluency, and reading comprehension. The results of these assessments were analyzed and indicated that she is meeting grade-level expectations for math and reading comprehension but is struggling or below grade-level expectations in reading fluency. Her teacher and grade level team use this data analysis to determine the appropriate instruction or interventions to help Eliza increase her reading fluency. Since this is an initial or beginning of the year assessment, the teacher and team may decide to wait and see if quality Tier 1 instruction is sufficient for remediating the issue or may begin providing additional support based on her academic history. Either way, Eliza's progress in reading fluency is reassessed and monitored on an ongoing basis, and the results used to inform subsequent instruction and interventions. This progress monitoring indicates whether the instruction is working and Eliza is making progress or the instruction is not working and needs to be adjusted. Assessment data as evidence of the effectiveness of the instruction is foundational to MTSS and ensures that Eliza, and all students, are making adequate academic and behavioral progress.

Not all schools implement MTSS, which is more prevalent in elementary and middle schools than in high schools. Its use is not federally mandated, which allows schools to design the multi-tiered framework that best meets their needs and resources. This framework can differ in the number of tiers (such as four tiers rather than three), the assessments and curriculum used, and the types of instruction and interventions provided. The principle of MTSS, such as RTI, remains consistent regardless of the differences in numbers of tiers, assessments, and teaching. This chapter will discuss the most common framework, the three-tiered RTI. Its critical components though are fundamental to any quality education.

Before RTI, a structure for providing support for students who struggle existed as a pre-referral process for special education. The components of the previous pre-referral process are embedded into RTI, but RTI is a more proactive approach that encompasses all students and not just those that may require special education services. It was developed to promptly identify students who struggle and provide early intervention services to prevent inappropriate referrals to special education.

Students may receive special education services without progressing through the tiers of RTI, especially students with medical or other conditions identified before elementary school. More information about the referral and eligibility processes for special education will be provided in Chapter 3.

RTI is a team-based approach requiring collaboration among school personnel. Rather than a general or special education program, it is a school-wide initiative designed to meet students' academic and behavioral needs. It fosters professional development among teachers by emphasizing brainstorming, sharing ideas, and problem solving. A general education teacher may identify a behavioral approach that works best while the special education teacher may discover an accommodation or assistive technology that better supports students. By working together and sharing resources, the team of professionals can learn and better meet the diverse learning and behavioral needs of all students (Shapiro, n.d.).

Comprehension Check

1   Describe the basic framework of MTSS.
2   Identify the role of assessment in the MTSS process.
3   Discuss why MTSS is considered a team-based approach rather than a general education or special education initiative.

Tiers of RTI

Tier 1

In RTI, Tier 1 is considered the "typical" general education classroom. Instruction is provided primarily by a qualified general education teacher and aligned to the individual state's academic or student learning standards. The curriculum and materials used are research-validated to be effective in teaching the designated subject matter. Publishers have validated most curriculums currently used in schools, and many districts have a specialist responsible for identifying the appropriate curriculum for their schools' needs and resources. Teacher preparation programs, such as those provided by accredited universities, and state education departments ensure teachers meet a level of competence through designated coursework, curriculum, and licensure procedures. These processes help ensure that students are instructed by a qualified teacher using a valid curriculum so that all students receive an appropriate instruction. In turn, this minimizes the possibility that a lack of student progress is due to poor instruction and is more likely the result of actual learning difficulties.

Classrooms consist of a wide range of students with diverse learning and behavioral challenges, and approximately 75–80% of them receive adequate instruction in Tier 1 (Shapiro, n.d.). In a class of 20, four or five students typically need supplementary education. These support services may be "pushed in" or "pulled out," meaning Tiers 2 and 3 services are provided either in the general education classroom or in a resource room. In the "pushed in" or inclusion model, the special education teacher, reading specialist, or other professional provides services, possibly through co-teaching, within the general education classroom. Additional information on co-teaching is in Chapter 7. It is important to remember that students in Tiers 2 and 3 struggle throughout the school day and may need additional supports to be successful. Instructional approaches such as Universal Design for Learning and appropriate accommodations may help provide that support. Collaboration with school personnel, parents, caregivers, and others is also critical in determining the approaches that offer the greatest success.

Students with disabilities may have mandated accommodations identified in Individualized Education Programs (IEP) or 504 plans for classroom and assessment purposes. Accommodations identified on these documents must be implemented as directed, including in the general education classroom. IEPs and 504 plans are discussed in greater detail in Chapters 5 and 6.

Since MTSS frameworks differ depending on the school, district, and individual teachers and students, there is no definitive point that identifies when students are referred to Tiers 2 and 3. Determining when a student needs additional support for reading fluency, comprehension, writing, math skills, or behavior may differ depending on the school, the district, and even teachers themselves. This is especially true for behavioral competencies and expectations. Generally, the research-validated curricula used in a school include progress monitoring assessments that can be used to identify students who are making adequate progress, are somewhat below expectations, and those at-risk or in need of additional support. Individual teachers' expectations and the degree of student progress though impacts the referral points for each tier.

Teacher expectations are important because it is possible in some schools, some or even many students could be performing below curricula benchmarks for adequate progress (e.g., due to high levels of poverty). The benchmarks identified by publishers for ranking how students are progressing are referenced to average performances of nationwide student samples and may be less indicative of averages with any local group of students. For example, some students, in a neighborhood school with high poverty levels, may have fewer quality pre-school and kindergarten experiences than in other neighborhoods. The 1st grade teachers are aware of this situation and understand that a number of students may initially be lagging in progress but should "catch up" over time. They are not alarmed to discover lower than average performances at the outset of the school year. Students are typically referred when the teacher and supporting evidence indicate that a student is not making adequate progress. See Case Study 2.1.

Case Study 2.1 Tier 1 Application

Ms. Tillerman is a general education teacher at Winchester School with a class of 22 students. At the beginning of the year, the school conducted a universal screening in reading fluency and established a benchmark of 100 words per minute (wpm). Students scoring less than 100 words per minute were progress monitored and reassessed on an ongoing basis. While the majority of Ms. Tillerman's student scored at or above the benchmark, six of her students did not.

Name	Sept 15 wpm
LaQuita B.	83
Christopher E.	56
Jaidyn G.	43
Ezekiel L.	79
Roberto M.	67
Samantha T.	83

Christopher and Jaidyn were previously identified with a learning disability and were receiving additional services in Language Arts. School records indicate that LaQuita and Ezekiel both struggled with fluency last year, but neither were referred for additional services. Roberto and Samantha are both new to the school, and their school records do not indicate previous fluency rates.

Ms. Tillerman analyzed the data and decided to reassess the six students in one month. She wanted to determine whether "summer slide" or being out of school for the last three months impacted the students' scores. She felt a month would also give her some time to get to know her students and their learning styles.

After one month she reassessed the students and received the following scores:

Name	Sept 15 wpm	Oct 17 wpm
LaQuita B.	83	102
Christopher E.	56	64
Jaidyn G.	43	62
Ezekiel L.	79	82
Roberto M.	67	74
Samantha T.	83	84

- Analyze the amount of growth for each student from September 15 to October 17. Which students do you believe are making adequate progress? Which ones are not?
- What additional information would be beneficial for Ms. Tillerman to learn about each student?
- Which, if any, students should Ms. Tillerman refer for Tier 2 support? Why?

Tier 2

When a student fails to make adequate progress either academically or behaviorally (including classroom, social, and functional behaviors) in Tier 1, they may be referred for additional support and possibly Tier 2 services. Typically, this process begins with a referral from the general education teacher after they have implemented all known viable interventions and tried everything they can to help a student. Teachers implement strategies and interventions in Tier 1 that go above and beyond what is provided for a typically progressing student, consult with parents, and document a student's lack of adequate progress. Any concerned adult with knowledge of the student can also initiate referrals (parents, guardians, caregivers, doctors).

A referral to Tier 2 does not mean that a student will eventually need or receive special education services. This tier offers assistance to students who do not qualify for special education but need extra help. While some students may eventually require Tier 3, the intent is to reduce the number of referrals through early intervention. Tier 2 is considered a pre-referral process meaning it occurs before a referral to special education is necessary to prevent such a referral if possible.

Tier 2 is a team-based approach, and once a referral is made, a meeting is arranged with the school's support team. This team has a variety of different names depending on the school and district, such as a Tier 2 support team, child study team, problem-solving team, pre-referral team, or intervention assistance team. All schools should have a support team that allows all teachers to receive additional support to address student concerns. In this text, this team is referred to as an intervention assistance team or IAT. The IAT helps students who may eventually receive Tier 2 support but is also a resource for all teachers in any grade or tier in need of additional assistance in addressing students' academic or behavioral needs.

An IAT is a team of professionals within the school that collaborates to resolve academic and behavioral struggles. This team typically has both permanent and temporary members depending on the needs of the student, teacher, and school. Permanent members may include administrators, school psychologists, counselors, and regular and general education teachers. These permanent members make up the core of the team and are typically involved in most IAT concerns. The temporary members are those most directly involved with the student of interest. They may consist of the student's general education teacher, grade level special education teacher, the student's parents, previous teachers, and possibly the student themselves. This team gathers information and works to identify appropriate interventions.

The referring teacher provides information about the area(s) of concern or target behavior(s), student background information, previous interventions implemented, their degree of success, and the goal or desired outcome. The IAT helps achieve the desired result by providing additional instructional strategies, resources, behavior intervention plans, consultations, or other support to help the student succeed (such as counseling, peer mentoring ...). See Table 2.1 for a sample Intervention Assistance Team Referral form.

The IAT team gathers data to identify the student's strengths, patterns of behavior, and areas of concern. This assessment process tends to be less formal than a referral to Tier 3 or special education, but it is essential in determining the appropriate interventions. Since general education teachers primarily initiate referrals to the IAT, there tends to be

Table 2.1 Intervention Assistance Team Referral Form

Intervention Assistance Team Referral Form	
Student's name:	Grade:
The person making the referral:	
Students areas of strengths:	
Circle the primary area of concern	
Math reading writing behavior social/emotional health including vision and hearing	
Description of the area(s) of concern citing specific evidence such as assessments, classroom work, and observational data	
Specific area of concern	**Supporting evidence (assessments, classroom work/performance, observational data)**
Identify three interventions previously implemented and the degree of success.	
Interventions previously implemented	**Degree of success**
1.	
2.	
3.	
Identify the desired outcome or goal for the intervention.	
School history, student background, medications or other necessary information	

classroom and assessment data to support and document the area of concern. In terms of academics, this information should include both summative and formative assessment data. Summative data such as low results on a standardized achievement test or a failing chapter test can provide the IAT with general areas of concern. However, summative assessment results often do not provide sufficient details in determining specific areas of strength and need. Formative assessment data, such as fluency tests, progress monitoring, or repeated measures of a specific skill, and class assignments, may provide a more detailed picture of the student's needs and abilities (Lamar-Duke & Dukes, 2005). Observations of the student's classroom behavior may be conducted as part of this data gathering process, especially for referrals with behavioral concerns.

Observations conducted by a third party (rather than the classroom teacher) tend to be more informative as it is difficult, if not impossible, to do a detailed student observation while teaching a class. A neutral third party, such as a special education teacher, a different general education teacher, school administrator, or counselor, typically provides a more objective view of the classroom dynamics and student behavior. Observations may assist in determining the cause or purpose of a student's action. They can provide additional information such as time on task, frequency, or duration of behaviors and the classroom dynamics that may be positively or negatively impacting the student. This information is used to determine replacement behaviors, strategies, teaching processes, instruction, and interventions.

Other assessment information may include a review of school records, hearing and vision screenings, medical history, interest inventories, and interviews with previous teachers, parents, and even the student themselves. Parent involvement is critical to the process to gain valuable insight and foster positive and collaborative relationships. See Case Study 2.2.

Case study 2.2 Referral to Tier 2

Taylor is a student at Willow Creek School and referred to the IAT by her teacher, Mr. Goetz, for academic and behavioral difficulties. Academically Taylor struggles in reading fluency and comprehension. Her summative assessments or grade-level standardized tests indicate that she performs below the established benchmarks in fluency and reading comprehension. According to Mr. Goetz, Taylor's formative assessment data consists of classroom assignments and observations that also indicate that she struggles in reading. Mr. Goetz reported that when asked to read independently in class, Taylor often appears off-task daydreaming, playing with objects at her desk, or distracting her peers. Taylor also has difficulty following teacher directions and has multiple incomplete and missing assignments. See Table 2.2 for a copy of Mr. Goetz IAT referral form.

Table 2.2 Intervention Assistance Team Referral Form – Johnson, Taylor

Intervention Assistance Team Referral Form	
Student's name: Taylor Johnson Grade:	
The person making the referral:	

Student's areas of strengths:

Gets along well with peers
Completes most math assignments, including homework, on time (9 out of 10 completed and turned in on time)
Stronger in math – especially math that does not involve word problems

Circle **the primary area of concern**

Math   <u>reading</u>   writing   <u>behavior</u>   social/emotional health including vision and hearing

Description of the area(s) of concern citing specific evidence such as assessments, classroom work, and observational data

Specific area of concern	Supporting evidence (assessments, classroom work/performance, observational data)
Reading Fluency	Often struggles reading passages aloud in class. Current reading fluency rate of 74 wpm (class average is 110 wpm)
Reading Comprehension	Scored 30% on recent classroom assessment, answering 3 out of 5 literal comprehension questions and 0 out of five figurative comprehension questions correctly.
Time off-task/missing assignments	Often appears off-task during work time (daydreaming, talking to a peer, playing with objects) and is currently missing 4 out of 7 in-class reading assignments.
Following directions	She takes significantly longer to follow teacher directions than her peers. Yesterday I asked her three times to get out her reading book before she complied.

Identify three interventions previously implemented and the degree of success.

Interventions previously implemented	Degree of success
1. Moved Taylor's seat to the front of the class	This has been somewhat successful in reducing the class time spent talking to peers instead of working. It has not helped in her completing more assignments.
2. Additional prompting and help	Somewhat successful. When I provide additional help (often one on one), Taylor is more successful in completing the assignments. She rarely asks for help, though, and usually waits until I come to her.
3. Peer tutoring	This did not seem to be successful. While the assignments were completed, the peer did the majority of the work, and Taylor copied the answers.

(continued)

Table 2.2 (continued)

Identify the desired outcome or goal for the intervention.
Increase Taylor's reading and comprehension level (or provide the appropriate support) so that she can complete assignments independently.
For Taylor to follow directions and pay attention in class
School history, student background, medications or other necessary information
Taylor is new to Willow Creek, and her previous school records are incomplete. While prior report cards grades are available, past assessment results are missing. Her previous year report card grades in language arts were all Ds while other content areas were primarily Bs and Cs.
The screenings completed this fall indicated she was below benchmark levels in fluency (68 wpm with a benchmark of 100 wpm) and comprehension (overall score of 76 with a class average of 97).
I have no knowledge or information about prior behavioral concerns.

> Review Mr. Goetz's IAT referral form and answer the following questions:
>
> - Who should be included in the IAT for Taylor?
> - What additional assessment information should the IAT gather and analyze before determining interventions?
> - What suggestions or strategies would you recommend Mr. Goetz implement in his classroom to better support Taylor?

Once the assessment information is compiled, it is analyzed and accurately defines the root or cause of the problem to address it appropriately. For example, if a student struggles with reading fluency, it is essential to determine, if possible, the cause or reason for this struggle, such as language processing issues, lack of phonemic awareness, visual problems, or other physical, social, emotional, or environmental concerns. Determining the source helps define the problem area and assists in establishing the appropriate goal and corresponding intervention. The goal and interventions for fluency issues for a student with a vision problem will be different from a student who exhibits a lack of phonemic awareness or difficulties focusing. The analysis allows the team to align the intervention with the specific needs of the student.

Once the assessment data is analyzed, the team establishes a goal and plan for the appropriate intervention and accommodations. This plan should measurably and objectively define the target behavior and acceptable or expected degree of progress.

In Tier 2, instruction is aligned to the student (rather than the whole class) and provided by either the general education teacher, special education teacher, or other specialists (such as reading specialist, behavioral consultant ...) within the general education classroom or in a separate resource room. The person responsible for providing the services and the location depends on the student's needs and the resources available within the school.

There are two main approaches to providing instruction in Tier 2, the problem-solving approach and standard protocol. Both have advantages and disadvantages, and the strengths of one are the weakness of the other and vice versa. The problem-solving approach determines individualized interventions to meet a specific student's needs but requires more time and resources. The standard protocol uses existing school structures and resources to meet the student's needs more generally but requires less time and fewer resources (Shapiro, 2009).

For example, Amelia is in 5th grade at the JT Murray Elementary School. Academically, she is stronger in reading but referred to the IAT for her struggles in mathematics. The JT Murray School uses a problem-solving approach in providing Tier 2 services. When analyzing her assessment data, the team determined that she appears to understand the form and procedures but is struggling with basic math facts. She typically knows how to solve problems but often gets incorrect answers due to errors in basic math facts. For example, in a recent work sample consisting of five-word problems, she incorrectly multiplied 7 x 6 (48), 8 x 4 (24), and divided 81 by 9 and got 8, but correctly identified key-words and the proper process. She knew what to do but still got the incorrect answers. The team determined the cause and identified specific instruction and interventions that focused on strategies for solving basic math problems in addition (counting on, doubles and near doubles, front end addition), subtraction (related equations, particle subtraction, compensation strategy), multiplication (repeat addition, partial products, counting up), and division (repeat subtraction, skip counting). She was also provided accommodations (addition and multiplication charts, open number lines) and taught how to use them. This process was time-consuming and required the school to have the available resources to provide individualized instruction to Amelia. The designated interventions, though, directly align to her specific needs, thus increasing the chances they will be successful and Amelia will reach her Tier 2 goal.

The standard protocol approach requires less time and resources, but the interventions are less likely to be directly aligned to the student's needs (Shapiro, 2009). For example, Jerome is a 6th-grader at the Jaidyn F. Christopher School and referred to the IAT for his struggles with reading comprehension. The team's analysis of his assessment data indicated that he was well below average in terms of figurative comprehension and below average in literal comprehension. The team determined that Jerome's difficulties were not due to issues with hearing, vision, or reading fluency. The Jaidyn F. Christopher School has a standard protocol for all reading issues. It uses a pre-established research-validated reading intervention program that addresses both fluency and comprehension. This approach provides instruction that somewhat aligns with Jerome's needs. He struggles with comprehension but not fluency. Jerome is more likely to begin receiving services sooner than through the problem-solving approach since the resources and curriculum are predetermined and available. The standard protocol requires less time and fewer resources, but the interventions may be less aligned to the student's actual needs. This may result in fewer successful interventions and lead to more students referred to Tier 3 services.

The advantages of one approach are the disadvantages of the other. To mitigate these effects, some schools choose to use the standard protocol for Tier 2 and the problem-solving approach in Tier 3. This combined approach meets the general needs of students in Tier 2 and provides additional individualized interventions for those who continue to struggle in Tier 3 (Shapiro, 2009).

In each approach, the student is reassessed and their progress monitored regularly to ensure that the intervention is successful. If adequate progress is being made, then the student typically remains in Tier 2 until the area of concern is remediated, and the established goal is achieved. If the progress monitoring results indicate that the student is not making progress, additional or different interventions may be implemented, or the team determines that a referral to Tier 3 is necessary.

Tier 3

The referral processes for Tier 1 to Tier 2 and Tier 2 to Tier 3 are similar, but there are specific procedures, timelines, and criteria for determining a student's eligibility for Tier 3 and special education. The eligibility process begins after a student fails to make adequate progress in Tier 2, and the team believes the student may qualify for special education services. The policies and procedures that guide the eligibility process are federally mandated under the Individuals with Disabilities Education Improvement Act (IDEA). IDEA details this process and guarantees six main provisions to students who qualify with a disability in one or more of the identified categories. The components of IDEA (Chapter 1), including the eligibility process (Chapter 3), disabilities (Chapter 4), and Individualized Education Programs (Chapter 5), will be discussed in greater detail throughout this book.

Most students who receive services through Tier 3 or special education spend most of their school day in the general education classroom under the guidance of a general education teacher. There are no special "tricks" for teaching students with disabilities. The qualities that make a successful teacher and the fundamentals for effective instruction for an inclusive classroom environment (such as Universal Design for Learning) are the same for all students, including those with disabilities and other diverse learning needs. Instructional strategies for students in Tier 3 may differ from that in a typical general education class in terms of individualization, pacing, curriculum, accommodations, supports, and time. Still, the fundamentals of effective teaching remain the same.

As suggested earlier, some schools may use four tiers in RTI. In those cases, Tier 3 is intensive, often individualized, instruction toward specific learning outcomes based on student needs. The four-tier model tends to make a delineation between those intensive interventions and the actual referral and identification for special education. Three-tiered models may also include more intensive and individualized instruction that occurs prior to the actual referral for special education. Do not be confused, whether there are three or four tiers, the purpose is to make every effort to address the student's need *prior* to actual referral.

Comprehension Check

1 Describe the purpose of each tier in RTI.
2 Describe the referral process from Tier 1 to Tier 2.
3 Explain the purpose of Tier 2 and the IAT.

Ongoing Cycle of Assessment

All tiers of MTSS and effective instruction, in general, are based on an ongoing cycle of assessment, analysis, decision making, and instruction (see Figure 2.1). This process provides teachers with the tools to implement data-driven instruction. Data-driven instruction uses prior assessment data to inform subsequent instruction. Therefore, instruction is based on an analysis of what students know and do not know based on specific assessment results. This ongoing cycle aligns instruction and content to the students' needs.

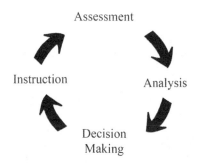

Figure 2.1 Ongoing Cycle

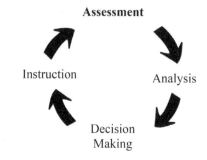

Assessment

Instruction   Analysis

Decision
Making

Figure 2.2 Ongoing Cycle: Assessment

Assessment: Universal Screening

The ongoing cycle begins with a universal screening or an initial assessment (see Figure 2.2) given to all students at the beginning of the school year to determine students' strengths and needs. This screening is not the sole indicator of who needs help and alone does not provide sufficient data to qualify a student for Tier 2. Students whose results are below the expected norms are progress monitored to ensure adequate academic growth and provided early intervention if necessary. The universal screenings are typically re-administered at least one to three times per year to ensure all students are making sufficient progress (Center on Response to Intervention, n.d.).

While MTSS offer support for both academic and behavioral concerns, universal screenings are typically only conducted in academic areas. Standardized behavioral screenings often require greater student knowledge than the teacher has at the beginning of the year. These assessments are also undertaken individually and require a great deal of time to complete on a classroom-wide basis. Teachers often use informal classroom observation to identify behavioral strengths and concerns and those in need of additional behavioral support.

Analysis

For assessment data to be beneficial, it must be analyzed to determine specific strengths, needs, baselines, and patterns of performance (see Figure 2.3). Whole groups (all 3rd graders), subgroups (gender, ethnicity, students with disabilities), and individual student results are analyzed to determine patterns and ensure that all students receive the necessary instruction and support. Analyzing the data helps teachers and schools assess what is working for which students and what is not working or needs to be adjusted (NAESP, n.d.)

As part of this process, schools and teachers often identify appropriate benchmarks or expected performance levels. For instance, a school may

Figure 2.3 Ongoing Cycle: Analysis

set a benchmark for reading fluency. Any student whose reading fluency is below the benchmark may be progress monitored to ensure adequate growth. Benchmarks may also be rank-ordered and provide a specific number or percentage of students' additional support. For instance, schools may rank order students and provide additional monitoring or support for those below the established percentile (the lowest 10% of students) rather than setting a specific criterion (a fluency level of 85 words per minute). This provides schools with specific criteria for judging performance and making instructional decisions based on data from and knowledge of their students (The IRIS Center, 2016; Lawless Frank, Christman, Baldwin, & Richards, 2018).

Decision Making

Once the assessment data is analyzed, it is used as evidence for instructional decisions (see Figure 2.4) to ensure the appropriate curriculum, instructional programs, and staffing levels. If the analysis indicates that students are improving, then the decision may be to continue the current instructional process and standards of progress monitoring. If the

Figure 2.4 Ongoing Cycle: Decision Making

analysis suggests students are not making adequate growth, then the decision may be to change or adjust educational components in some way to better meet students' needs (Lawless Frank et al., 2018; NAESP, n.d.).

Instruction

The final step in the ongoing cycle is to provide data-driven instruction (see Figure 2.5) by a qualified teacher using a valid curriculum. Using assessment evidence to guide this process ensures that students are provided with the best opportunity to make the appropriate academic and behavioral gains. Instruction should not be the first step in the process but an informed decision based on specific evidence of what the student knows and is able to do.

The instruction, curriculum, and interventions provided to all students in all tiers should be research-validated. This means that when implemented as directed, research has shown it to be effective in teaching students a particular skill or concept. In Tier 1, the teacher provides this instruction to the entire class. In Tiers 2 and 3, the student to teacher ratio tends to be much smaller (typically five to eight students in Tier 2 and three to five students in Tier 3), allowing for more individualized attention and instructional alignment to the students' needs (Lawless Frank, et al., 2018; Nellis, 2012; NJCLD, 2005).

Instruction may also differ in terms of amount of time, frequency, pacing, and instructional materials. Students with more intense needs may require more instructional time, such as additional math instructions two days per week in Tier 2 and four days in Tier 3. The pacing of instruction may also be slower, allowing more practice of skills and time for students to process the information. Accommodations such as speech to text software for writing, text to speech for reading, and different instructional materials (including addressing adaptive living or functional skills) may be used to meet students' needs.

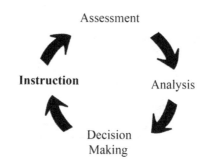

Figure 2.5 Ongoing Cycle: Instruction

Progress Monitoring

The ongoing cycle does not stop at instruction. The process continues with progress monitoring or reassessments of the same skills to ensure that students continue to achieve. A key to the cycle's effectiveness is that the same specific skill is monitored. For example, the math skills assessed, such as the rate and accuracy of single-digit multiplication, are the same skills reassessed and progress monitored. Classroom grades, assignments, and chapter tests assess different knowledge and skills each time; therefore, they may not always assess the targeted skills to be learned by any given student. Progress monitoring assesses the same skill on a regular basis. In Tiers 2 and 3, skills are monitored more frequently, such as every two weeks, or bi-monthly.

MTSS increase student growth through data-driven instruction provided by a qualified teacher using a valid curriculum, and thus increase levels of support based on individual student needs using an ongoing cycle of assessment, analysis, decision making, and instruction. This cycle promotes informed decisions to enhance student growth, provide early intervention, and reduce inappropriate referrals to special education.

Comprehension Check

1   Describe the purpose of the ongoing assessment cycle used in RTI.
2   Identify each component of the ongoing cycle.
3   Explain the importance of continuing the use of the cycle throughout the school year.

References

Center on Response to Intervention. (n.d.). RTI implementer series [PowerPoint slides]. Retrieved from www.rti4success.org/resource/rti-implementer-series-m odule-1-screening.

The IRIS Center. (2016). Universal screening. Retrieved from http://iris.peabody. vanderbilt.edu/module/rti-math/cresource/q1/p03/#content.

Lamar-Dukes, P., & Dukes, C. (2005). Consider the roles and responsibilities of the inclusion support teacher. *Intervention in School and Clinic*, 41(1), 55–61.

Lawless Frank, C., Christman, J.T., Baldwin, J.L., & Richards, S.B. (2018). *Managing classroom and student behavior*. New York, NY: Routledge.

National Association of Elementary School Principals (NAESP). (n.d.). Student assessment: Using student achievement data to support instructional decision making. Retrieved from www.naesp.org/sites/default/files/Student%20Achievement_blue.pdf.

National Joint Committee on Learning Disabilities (NJCLD). (2005). Responsiveness to intervention and learning disabilities. Retrieved from www.ldonline. org/article/11498.

Nellis, L. (2012). Maximizing the effectiveness of building teams in response to intervention implementation. *Psychology in the Schools*, 49(3), 245–256.

Shapiro, E. S. (n.d.). Tiered instruction and intervention in a response to intervention model. Retrieved from www.rtinetwork.org/essential/tiered instruction/tiered-instruction-and-intervention-rti-model?tmpl=component&print=.

Shapiro, E. S. (2009). The two models of RTI: Standard protocol and problem solving. Bethlehem, PA. Retrieved from www.doe.virginia.gov/instruction/virginia_tiered_system_supports/response_intervention/two_models.pdf, 09/2015.

3 Assessment and Identification

Stephen B. Richards

Objectives: After reading the chapter, students will be able to:

1 Identify the roles and responsibilities of general educators in the referral process
2 Identify the roles and responsibilities of general and special educators in the multi-factor evaluation (MFE) process
3 Identify the types of data general educators may provide to the MDET
4 Identify what steps are included in determining whether a student is eligible for special education.

Chapter 1 discussed provisions under IDEA concerning nondiscriminatory evaluation for eligibility for special education and related services. Chapter 2 explained how MTSS, including RTI, are implemented, as well as progress monitoring of students' academic and behavioral performances, through an on-going cycle of assessment. The progress monitoring data is often the foundation for a referral for a multi-factor evaluation (MFE) for special education eligibility. Schools must rely on multiple sources of data provided by more than one professional to ensure the process is nondiscriminatory. Therefore, various professionals and parents are typically involved in the assessment and identification process through the multi-disciplinary evaluation team (MDET).

Role of the General and Special Educator

General education teachers play a primary role in the initial assessment for the identification process and throughout, including the development of an individualized education program (IEP). General educators have been involved in the MTSS process and team decisions and the on-going cycle of assessment. They are familiar with the student's background, classroom performance and behavior, social skills, communication abilities, and how well the student adjusts to changing demands in the classroom and other school environments. The general education teachers are often the first to identify the student as struggling, the first to convey concerns to parents, and implement interventions to alleviate the struggles in the general education classroom. Therefore, general educators are nearly always included as contributors to the assessment and identification processes from start to end. General education teachers typically provide data of various forms, make suggestions for other types of assessment, and evaluate data toward identification for special education. They are also involved in writing, implementing, and updating IEPs. IDEA includes a principle generally referred to as *child find*. This principle places responsibility on schools and educators to ensure students who may need special education are referred and evaluated for eligibility. The school cannot simply ignore a student struggling through the tiers of RTI and the MTSS. As a student progresses through an MTSS including RTI, special education teachers will likely be more involved with the student and will also be collecting data along with other team members (e.g., Intervention Assistance Teams as described in Chapter 2), particularly progress monitoring data.

The Referral

The referral for a multi-factor evaluation (MFE) may come from several sources, including an MTSS team (these teams may be referred to as Intervention Assistance Teams as discussed in Chapter 2, or Student Assistance Teams, Child Study Teams, or other names depending on the state). However, parents and agencies (e.g., Department of Health and Human Resources that serve children from birth–3 years of age) may also make a referral. Regardless of who makes the referral, parents must first be informed of their rights before continuing the process. States have procedural safeguard documents that explain these rights and the process in language accessible to parents (for instance, parents' native language). Parents must also give consent for the school to conduct an MFE. Figure 3.1 includes a state form to obtain consent for an MFE from parents or the student themselves if they are of legal age.

The Identification Process

Once a referral for evaluation for special education is made, several steps must occur. First, the MDET may include a general education teacher, special education teacher, school psychologist or diagnostician, administrator, parents, and any necessary related services personnel (e.g., speech and language pathologist, assistive technology specialist, occupational therapist). Other team members may also be included such as a psychologist hired by the family, medical personnel, or parent advocate. Based on the referral and existing data, the MDET members will decide what assessments and data are needed and who will conduct the evaluations and collect the data. Typically, the administrator facilitates the assessment process. There are many possible assessment areas including (but not limited to):

NOTICE OF INDIVIDUAL EVALUATION/REEVALUATION REQUEST

_____ **County Schools**

Student's Full Name _____ **Date** _____
School _____ **Date of Birth** _____
Parent(s)/Guardian(s) _____ **Grade** _____
Address _____ **WVEIS#** _____
City/State/Zip _____ **Telephone** _____

O
☐ **INITIAL**   ☐ **REEVALUATION**

Dear Parent(s)/Adult Student:

Your permission is requested to conduct an evaluation to determine the student's educational needs. If the student has been receiving special education services, a reevaluation is required at least every three years or more frequently, if warranted. Upon completion of the evaluation, a meeting will be scheduled to discuss the evaluation results.

This evaluation will be conducted by qualified professionals and will include the areas checked below. A written description of each evaluation component is provided. The evaluation results will be used as the primary source to determine the student's eligibility for special education and related services and/or to adjust the student's educational services.

☐ Academic Information	☐ Developmental Skills	☐ Perceptual-Motor
☐ Achievement	☐ Health	☐ Social Skills
☐ Classroom Performance	☐ Hearing/Audiological	☐ Transition Assessments
☐ Teacher Report	☐ Functional Listening Evaluation	☐ Functional Vocational Evaluation
☐ Adaptive Skills	☐ Information from the Parents	☐ Vocational Aptitudes
☐ Assistive Technology	☐ Intellectual Ability	☐ Interests/Preferences
☐ Behavioral Performance	☐ Motor Skills	☐ Vision
☐ Functional Behavioral Assessment	☐ Physical Therapy	☐ Orientation and Mobility
☐ Communication	☐ Occupational Therapy	☐ Observation(s)
☐ Other (specify) _____		

☐ **Procedural Safeguards Brochure** explaining parent/student rights and the responsibilities of the county school district is enclosed for an initial referral.

_____
Signature   Date

I have read, or had read to me, the above Notice of Individual Evaluation/Reevaluation Request regarding the student. I understand the contents and implications of this notice and have been advised of my rights.

Check one:
☐ I give permission to evaluate/reevaluate.
☐ I wish to schedule a conference before I decide.
☐ Do not evaluate/reevaluate the student.

```
* REQUIRED *
Received by school/county:
___/___/___        _____
   Date               Personnel
```

_____
Parent/Adult Student Signature   Date

Please return this signed form within 5 days and retain a copy for your records.

West Virginia Department of Education
March 2017

Figure 3.1 Notice of Evaluation Request

EVALUATION COMPONENTS

Academic Information – measures of student performance as demonstrated on formative and summative assessments.
    Achievement – individually administered standardized tests that measure a student's skills in a variety of academic areas.
        Examples: mathematics, reading, science and social studies
    Classroom Performance – information collected on the student's learning and progress in the classroom.
        Examples: end of the chapter tests, portfolio assessment, classroom-based assessment, progress-monitoring data, interim assessments, benchmark assessments
    Teacher Report – information provided by any or all of the student's current teachers
        Examples: information pertaining to a student's organizational skills, attention to task, work/study habits, grades

Adaptive Skills – measures to determine skills necessary to function adequately within a person's home, school or community environment.
        Examples: communication, self-care, home living, social skills, community use, self-direction, health and safety, functional academics, leisure and work

Assistive Technology – procedures to determine if a student requires devices or services to increase, maintain or improve functional capabilities.
        Examples: functional environmental evaluation to determine the need for devices including, but not limited to, a communication board, adapted equipment or computer software

Behavioral Performance – measures to determine a student's behavioral, social and/or affective status.
        Examples: conduct in the classroom, ability to attend or focus, self-concept, emotional functioning, relationships with others
    Functional Behavioral Assessment (FBA) – structured process to determine the possible functions of a student's behavior so interventions and modifications can be developed.
        Examples: systematic observations, data collection, interviews

Communication - measures to determine skills necessary to understand and express information.
        Examples: speech sounds, oral language, phonemic awareness, facial expressions, body movements, gestures, touch

Developmental Skills – procedures to determine the student's early learning and school readiness.
        Examples: developmental milestones in communication, motor, cognitive, social emotional, self-help

Health – acquisition of information to determine the effect of health concerns on educational performance.
        Examples: report of a medical diagnosis from a physician or health history

Hearing/ Audiological – measures to determine the student's ability to hear or process language.
    Functional Listening Evaluation – assess how a student's listening abilities are affected by noise, distance and visual input in the student's natural listening environment

Information from the Parents – acquisition of information from the parents to assist in evaluation and program planning.
        Examples: social/emotional, developmental history, student preferences, medical history, cultural influence, behavioral information

Intellectual Ability – individualized, standardized measures to assess a student's ability or potential to learn.
        Examples: perception, cognition, memory, processing speed, verbal and non-verbal skills

Motor Skills – measures to determine a student's gross and fine motor development.
        Examples: mobility, muscle tone, balance, coordination, accessibility

Observation(s) – a purposeful study in a variety of activities, situations and/or times at school, home or other settings.
        Examples: data collection of student behavior and/or performance in a variety of classes and/or unstructured settings

Perceptual-Motor – measures to determine the student's ability to convert what is seen to written form.
        Example: reproducing a pattern from a sample

Social Skills – measures to determine the student's ability to initiate and maintain positive relationships with others.
        Examples: making friends, problem-solving, cooperating with others, following rules, showing appreciation

Transition Assessments – a planned, continuous process of obtaining, organizing and using selected formal and informal information to assist students in decision-making and preparation for successfully meeting their goals and expectations from school to post-school activities.
    Functional Vocational Evaluation – real and simulated measures to determine a student's ability to perform certain aspects of a work-related task and may include a purposeful study of the student in a variety of work-related activities.
        Examples: hands-on work samples, progress reports, job performance checklists
    Vocational Aptitudes – measures to determine prerequisite abilities pertaining to the world of work.
        Examples: manual dexterity, proof reading words and numbers, color discrimination
    Interests/Preferences – measures to assist with post-secondary planning, including schooling, employment and adult living.
        Example: career assessment inventory

Vision – measures to determine the student's functional vision and/or physical eye conditions.
        Examples: ophthalmological, optometrist report
    Orientation and Mobility – assesses the ability of the student who is low vision, blind, or deafblind in the use of his/her remaining senses to determine his/her position in the environment and in techniques for safe movement from one place to another.
        Examples: concept development, pedestrian safety, cane skills, route planning

Other: Specify_____

West Virginia Department of Education
March 2017

Figure 3.1 (continued)

- Academic achievement
- Classroom performance
- Adaptive skills
- Assistive technology needs
- Behavioral performance
- Communication
- Developmental skills
- Health
- Hearing
- Parental input (e.g., developmental history)
- Intellectual ability
- Motor skills (fine and gross motor)
- Classroom observations
- Perceptual motor skills
- Social skills
- Vision
- Vocational aptitudes and interests.

Comprehension Check

1 Who makes a referral for an MFE?
2 Who are likely to be members of the MDET?
3 What areas might be assessed during the MFE?

General Educator and Data

The MTSS process data verifies a student is struggling in school. The MFE is implemented to obtain the data required to identify a student for special education under one of the disability categories under IDEA (e.g., specific learning disability, intellectual disability, autism; Appendix A includes specific eligibility criteria, Chapter 4 includes all the disability category definitions under IDEA). Two identification criteria that must be met regardless of the disability are: (1) the verification of an adverse effect on educational performance and (2) the need for special education.

Classroom-based Assessments

The general education teacher will have considerable data to assist in the identification process through the on-going cycle of assessment discussed in Chapter 2. This data most often focuses on academic progress in the general education curriculum aligned with college and career readiness standards. This data is vital in identifying a student for special education. Academic progress data typically is obtained through several different types of assessments. Portfolios of classroom performance (e.g., writing samples from various points in the school year, math work samples) provide an overview of a student's progress on teacher-made and curriculum-based assessments (i.e., district-adopted curricula in English language arts, math, etc.). They also often include the workbooks and lesson plan books the students work through during the year.

General education teachers also have valuable data regarding student academic and classroom behavior. Teachers often have informal, anecdotal data from observations and written notes that address how well a student pays attention, completes assignments, gets along with peers, follows directions, and myriad other aspects of a student's response to the demands of school. They generally have grades recorded and report cards to parents (typically every nine weeks of the school year) that provide insight into a student's overall progress. General education teachers may have notes and observations from parent–teacher conferences as well.

Progress Monitoring

As discussed in Chapter 2, MTSS requires regular monitoring of students' progress in each of the three tiers. In Tier 1, there is universal screening two or more times throughout the school year when all students are assessed in essential skills such as math, reading fluency, and comprehension. With younger students, progress monitoring data may be obtained frequently (e.g., weekly or bi-weekly), in Tiers 2 and 3, although there are no exact requirements under IDEA. This data may be gathered by the general education teacher and special education teacher or other personnel directly involved in educating the student. Progress monitoring at Tiers 2–3, depending on the grade level, might include:

- Letter and number identification
- Sound/symbol recognition
- Sight word vocabulary
- Fluency (correct words read per minute)
- Reading comprehension
- Number concepts
- Computational knowledge and skills
- Number of math problems solved correctly in a specific time period (math fluency)
- Social/behavioral rating scales
- Observational behavioral data (e.g., frequency of outbursts at school).

This list is not exhaustive of possible areas that might be monitored. The key is these assessments occur regularly, to determine how much progress a student is making, compared to class peers or national standards. Often students are classified through MTSS data within categories such as adequate progress, below target, at-risk, and so on compared to national standards (e.g., how many correct words per minute a 1st grader should be reading in spring of the 1st grade). The comparison to peers is important because the student's peers may also be below target, indicating an educational issue other than the learning of an individual student. Peer comparisons may be particularly important in schools where students experience at-risk factors such as higher rates of poverty, homelessness, or nutritional stress that may work to suppress achievement for many students.

General education teachers may also collect more formal relevant social, behavioral, and communication skill data, through observation and rating scales or checklists. For example, general education teachers may rate how well a student works with others, follows directions, achieves motor skills such as walking up and down stairs, and so forth. General education teachers may observe physical symptoms of an underlying disability (e.g., not hearing directions, difficulty seeing or reading, chronic fatigue, unusual thirst and urination that could implicate Type I diabetes, and signs and symptoms of autism). Case Study 3.1 will challenge you to think about data and what it might mean regarding instruction.

Case Study 3.1

Assume you are a 1st grade teacher and you are reviewing your 20 students' results from the second universal screening of reading fluency that was administered in December of the school year, just before the winter break. You notice the following results for your class:

Adequate Progress (29 or more correct words
read per minute)   = 2 students
Below Adequate (16–28 correct words read
per minute)   = 12 students
A-risk (fewer than 16 correct words read
per minute)   = 6 students

1   You are using a research-validated ELA curriculum but one
    being used in the district for the first time. What might explain
    such results?
2   Should the lower 6 students be referred for an MFE? Why or
    why not?

Finally, general education teachers administer (but do not score) state- and district-wide achievement tests as required. This data helps school districts determine individual student performances and class, group, school-wide, and district-wide academic achievement levels.

The MDET is not likely to use all types of informal and formal assessments on any one student, but the options are there. The initial suspected disability may or may not be the disability category under which the student is identified. Identifying a suspected category based on collected data, state achievement test scores, interventions, and progress monitoring offer guidance to the MDET regarding the appropriate assessments for the MDE.

For example, a suspected intellectual disability requires assessments of cognitive ability (often an IQ test) and adaptive skills (how well the person adjusts to and functions in communication, socialization, motor skills, personal skills). Individual achievement tests are typically administered as well as other assessments, such as a speech and language evaluation, and vision and hearing screenings. The assessments selected usually align with the definition of the suspected disability under IDEA and state law. Intellectual disability (ID) includes identifying significant sub-average cognitive functioning, existing concurrently with deficits in adaptive concepts and skills, and becoming apparent during the developmental period (birth to 18 years of age). Hence, MDETs will use cognitive ability tests and adaptive skills assessments if an ID is the suspected disability. Achievement tests and RTI data help establish an adverse effect on educational performance and a need for special education. Importantly, such assessments can also provide insight into educational interventions that have been successful with a student, areas to target for instruction, and how best to assess student progress. Each disability category has its requirements for data establishing eligibility for special education. Regardless of the suspected disability, there must be more than one source of data, and the MDET must include more than one person. General education teachers are typically members of the MDET and often have the best holistic knowledge of a student. General educators may also administer one or more MDET assessments, such as individual achievement tests (Frank, Christman, Baldwin, & Richards, 2019). Special education teachers often administer individual assessments as part of the MDET, as well as provide progress monitoring data from Tiers 2 and 3 interventions.

Comprehension Check

1 What types of classroom assessment data do general education teachers collect?
2 What is a progress monitoring assessment?
3 How does identifying a "suspected disability" help the MDET in the assessment process?

Determining Eligibility for Special Education

States adopt and publish policies and procedures, outlining specific guidelines and requirements for assessment, and identifying a student for eligibility for special education and related services. Generally, the following steps are used (summarized from West Virginia Policy 2419: Regulations for the Education of Students with Exceptionalities):

1 Parental input and consent must be obtained. Before the MDET can begin its work toward determining whether a student is eligible, parents must agree to go ahead with it. If parents do not consent, the student remains in general education classes and continues to receive support.

2 If parental consent is obtained, the MDET establishes its plans for an MFE. The MFE must be completed within 60 days of parental consent. Depending on state requirements, this timeline may be altered based on factors such as school holidays, weekends, etc. but cannot be delayed beyond the state's specific time frame for MFE completion.

3 The MDET establishes who will conduct the needed assessments and begins its work on the MFE. Many possible types of evaluations may be administered based on the suspected disability and in response to existing and new data obtained. However, the MDET uses *individual* assessments. Group screening or state-wide group achievement tests, for example, cannot be the primary sources of data.

4 Additional information may be gathered for eligibility for specific learning disabilities or autism, for example. This additional information ensures the required criteria for eligibility have been met. For specific learning disabilities, schools must document the student's struggles are not due to vision or hearing problems, an intellectual or emotional or behavioral disability, socioeconomic status, cultural or linguistic differences, or environment (e.g., not due to poor classroom instruction).

5 Once the MFE is concluded, the MDET (or sometimes an eligibility committee) analyzes the data from the multiple sources, provided by multiple individuals, and decides whether the student meets the criteria for one of the disability categories included under IDEA.

6 There must be data in the MFE to verify: (1) a disability exists, (2) that the disability has an adverse effect on educational performance, and (3) the disability results in a need for special education.

7 If the student is determined to be eligible for special education (e.g., as a student with a speech disorder, specific learning disability, emotional or behavioral disorder), the team must again obtain parental consent before implementing an IEP.

8 The IEP is written (given parental consent) and must be implemented within 30 days of the identification and eligibility meeting. Again, states may provide policies for slight modifications in this timeline based on actual days of school within the 30 days.

9 The IEP is implemented with goals and objectives, assessment procedures, and special education and related services identified along with various other components and considerations discussed in greater detail in Chapter 5.

10 IEPs must be reviewed at least annually, and parental consent obtained each year for continued special education.

11   MFEs are conducted every three years to establish continued eligibility for special education and to obtain new data and insight into how to develop and implement an IEP.

Not every student who is referred for an MFE will be determined to be eligible for special education, even when parents consent to and support the process. If one or more of the three conditions (i.e., a disability exists, has an adverse effect on educational performance, and requires special education) is not established, then the student is not considered eligible for special education.

As an example, many students in schools have vision problems. Any student might have hyperopia (far-sightedness), myopia (near-sightedness), astigmatism, or other visual issues. Still, the visual problem might be managed well through the use of corrective lenses, surgery, or other procedures. For most students, the vision problems do not have an adverse effect on educational performance or the need for special education. However, a minimal number of students do have sufficiently poor vision and meet all three criteria (poor vision, adverse effect on educational performance, and need for special education), even with the use of corrective lenses. Students who are identified as having a disability but not a need for special education may be provided with an accommodation (504) plan, as discussed in Chapters 1 and 6.

Appendix A includes a report form from an MFE/MDET to determine whether a student is eligible for special education (West Virginia Department of Education, 2017, Special Education Forms and Instructions, retrieved 05/2020). Appendix A should also be reviewed when reading Chapter 4 as the appendix lists very specific identification/eligibility criteria for each disability category in a compact format. Bear in mind these criteria may differ from state to state so readers are encouraged to visit their state's department of education website and review the MDET/Eligibility forms applicable.

Similarly, a student may perform below average in comparison to national standards but is achieving at an average level compared to the same class, school, or district peers. Such comparisons may indicate issues in providing education to all students, not any particular student. Not every student who has academic issues will be eligible for special education. Case Study 3.2 will challenge you to consider factors that might affect decisions to make a referral for an MFE.

Case Study 3.2

You are teaching in the 7th grade at a grades 7–8 school. You are part of a team that reviews the data and information concerning students who are in Tier 2 of RTI. Keisha is a general education student. You have already met with the other general education teachers who teach Keisha in the various content areas.

Each 7th grade teacher says they have noticed that Keisha is not focused as much as she should be. You have reviewed Keisha's school records from previous years and there has never been any significant mention of her having difficulties with paying attention, focusing, or following directions. Two of her general education teachers remark that she does not follow directions when given the first time and often raises her hand to ask the teacher to repeat the directions.

You have noticed Keisha doesn't converse with her peers as much as other students, particularly when in a large group. Similarly, she doesn't usually volunteer to comment during class discussions.

You have contacted Keisha's parents and they also have noticed she seems to pay less attention to what they tell her than in the past. They are concerned that her grades are starting to suffer and she seems to spend more time alone. Her parents also say it can be annoying when she says "Huh?" and "What" so often in response to their questions or comments. What would you recommend to the team as next steps in addressing Keisha's issues?

1   Would you consider asking the team to begin the referral process for an MFE for Keisha? Why or why not?

Finally, general education teachers participate in the development and implementation of IEPs, monitoring progress on IEP goals and objectives, and providing services and accommodations specified in the IEP. A determination of eligibility and implementation of special education does not necessarily mean a student will be "removed" from the general education classroom or be less engaged in the general education college and career readiness curriculum. Most students identified for special education still spend 50% or more of their school day in the same classrooms as they would if they were not identified in special education (Smiley, Richards, & Taylor, 2019). Students in special education are educated in their least restrictive environment (LRE) as determined by the IEP team, alongside their nondisabled peers to the maximum extent *appropriate*.

Comprehension Check

1   List and discuss the three requirements for identification and services under IDEA.
2   What steps in the identification process require parental consent?
3   Discuss why a student identified as having a disability may not require special education.

Appendix A

ELIGIBILITY COMMITTEE REPORT

_____County Schools

Student Full Name _____	**Date** _____
School _____	**Date of Birth** _____
Parent(s)/Guardian(s) _____	**Grade** _____
Address _____	**WVEIS #** _____
City/State/Zip _____	**Telephone** _____

☐ Initial   ☐ Reevaluation

The Eligibility Committee (EC) considered the following multi-disciplinary reports and other relevant information.

☐ Academic Information
  ☐ Achievement
  ☐ Classroom Performance
  ☐ Teacher Report
☐ Adaptive Skills
☐ Assistive Technology
☐ Behavioral Performance
  ☐ Functional Behavioral Assessment
☐ Communication

☐ Developmental Skills
☐ Health_____
☐ Hearing
☐ Information from the Parents
☐ Intellectual Ability
☐ Motor Skills
☐ Observation(s)
☐ Perceptual-Motor

☐ Social Skills
☐ Transition Assessments
  ☐ Functional Vocational Evaluation
  ☐ Vocational Aptitudes
  ☐ Interests/Preferences
☐ Vision
  ☐ Orientation and Mobility
☐ Other _____

A student *cannot be identified* as a student in need of special education services if the primary reason for the decision is due to any of the following:

- A lack of appropriate instruction in the essential components of reading; or
- A lack of instruction in mathematics; or
- Limited English proficiency

For initial evaluation or reevaluation, the student meets the three-prong test of eligibility:
  ☐ Meets the eligibility requirements for one of the specific exceptionalities; **and**
  ☐ Experiences an adverse effect on educational performance; **and**
  ☐ Needs special education.

For reevaluation only:
  If a student no longer meets the eligibility criteria in one of the designated exceptionalities, the EC must provide the justification for continued eligibility. _____

The Eligibility Committee has determined the student's primary area of exceptionality is (only one):

☐ Autism (AU)
☐ Emotional/Behavioral Disorders (BD)
☐ Blindness and Low Vision (VI)*
☐ Deafblindness (DB) *
☐ Deafness (DF) *
☐ Hard of Hearing (HI) *

☐ Exceptional Gifted (EG)
☐ Gifted (GF)
☐ Orthopedic Impairment (PH)
☐ Other Health Impairment (OH)
☐ Intellectual Disability (Designate WVEIS Code ☐MM ☐MD ☐MS)

☐ Developmental Delay (PS)
☐ Specific Learning Disability (LD)
☐ Speech/Language Impairment (CD)
☐ Traumatic Brain Injury (TB)
☐ None

* Provide information pertaining to the West Virginia Schools for the Deaf and Blind.

Additional evaluation data are needed in the following areas: _____

The Eligibility Committee has determined the student is not eligible for special education and submits the following recommendations for consideration by the school team (e.g., SAT or instruction and intervention team): _____

Eligibility Committee Members

Signature	Position
_____	Administrator/Principal/Designee
_____	Evaluator/Specialist
_____	General and/or Special Educator
_____	Parent/Guardian/Adult Student
_____	Student
_____	Other _____

West Virginia Department of Education
March 2017

ELIGIBILITY DETERMINATION CHECKLIST

Student's Name: _____   Date of EC Meeting _____

The Eligibility Committee (EC) must consider all eligibility criteria relevant to any suspected exceptionalities.

A. **Autism - Documentation the student meets Criteria one (1) through five (5) as specified:**
    Documentation will assure that the student meets all of Section A and at least two (2) criteria from Section B and meets Sections C, D and E.
___ **Criterion 1:**
    ___ Section A. Persistent deficits in social communication and social interaction across multiple contexts, as manifested by the following currently or by history.
      1. ___ Deficits in social-emotional reciprocity, ranging, for example, from abnormal social approach and failure of normal back-and-forth conversation; to reduced sharing of interests, emotions or affect; to failure to initiate or respond to social interactions.
      2. ___ Deficits in nonverbal communicative behaviors used for social interaction, ranging, for example, from poorly integrated verbal and nonverbal communication; to abnormalities in eye contact and body language or deficits in understanding and use of gestures; to a total lack of facial expressions and nonverbal communication.
      3. ___ Deficits in developing, maintaining and understanding relationships, ranging, for example, from difficulties adjusting behavior to suit various social contexts; to difficulties in sharing imaginative play or in making friends; to absence of interest in peers.
    ___ Section B. Restricted repetitive and stereotyped patterns of behavior, interests and activities, as manifested by at least two of the following: Indicate when behavioral characteristics are/were evident. Two of the four eligibility criteria must be met.
      4. ___ Stereotypical or repetitive motor movements, use of objects or speech (e.g., simple motor stereotypies, lining up toys or flipping objects, echolalia, idiosyncratic phrases).
      5. ___ Insistence on sameness, inflexible adherence to routines or ritualized patterns or verbal and nonverbal behavior (e.g., extreme distress at small changes, difficulties with transitions, need to take same route or eat same food every day).
      6. ___ Highly restricted, fixated interests that are abnormal in intensity or focus (e.g., strong attachment to or preoccupation with unusual objects, excessively circumscribed or perseverative interest).
      7. ___ Hyper- or hypo-reactivity to sensory input or unusual interests in sensory aspects of the environment (e.g., apparent indifference to pain/temperature, adverse response to specific sounds or textures, excessive smelling or touching of objects, visual fascination with lights or movement).
    ___ Section C. Although symptoms for children with autism are typically present in the early development, some symptoms may not become fully manifest until social demands exceed limited capacities. Please attach an explanation.
      NOTE: IDEA regulations state "A child who manifests the characteristics of autism after age three could be identified as having autism," if all other criteria are satisfied.
    ___ Section D. Symptoms cause clinically significant impairment in social, occupational or other important areas of current functioning
    ___ Section E. These disturbances are not better explained by intellectual disability or global developmental delay.
___ **Criterion 2:**
    The student is diagnosed as having autism by a psychiatrist, physician, licensed psychologist or school psychologist and the evaluation report is attached.
___ **Criterion 3:**
    The student's condition adversely affects educational performance.
___ **Criterion 4:**
    The student needs special education.
___ **Criterion 5:**
    The student's educational performance is not adversely affected primarily because the student has an emotional/behavioral disorder as defined in Policy 2419.

B. **Blindness and Low Vision - Documentation the student meets ALL of the following:**
    1. ___ The student has a documented visual impairment, not primarily perceptual in nature, as determined by an optometrist or ophthalmologist or neurologist:
      a. ___ Measured acuity of 20/70 or less in the better eye with correction at distance or near;
      b. ___ Visual field restriction of twenty degrees or less in the better eye;
      c. ___ A deteriorating eye condition which will result in loss of visual efficiency (e.g., glaucoma, retinitis pigmentosa, or macular degeneration); or
      d. ___ A visual loss caused by a disturbance of the posterior visual pathway and/or cortex.
      e. ___ Functional Visual Assessment determined limited visual access or ability.
    2. ___ The student's physical eye condition, even with correction, adversely affects educational performance.
    3. ___ The student needs special education.

C. **Deafblindness - Documentation the student meets ALL of the following:**
    1. ___ The student exhibits characteristics consistent with the definition.
    2. ___ The student is diagnosed by an optometrist or ophthalmologist for vision loss and by an otologist, otolaryngologist, or audiologist for hearing loss.
    3. ___ The student's condition adversely affects educational performance.
    4. ___ The student needs special education.

D. **Deafness - Documentation the student meets ALL of the following:**
    1. ___ The student exhibits characteristics consistent with the definition and relies primarily on vision to access spoken communication.
    2. ___ The student has been diagnosed by an otologist, otolaryngologist, or audiologist as having a hearing loss.
    3. ___ The student's condition adversely affects educational performance.
    4. ___ The student needs special education.

E. **Developmental Delay - Documentation the student meets ALL of the following:**
    1. ___ Documentation the student is functioning at or lower than 75% of the normal rate of development in **two** or more of the following areas:
      a. ___ Cognition
      b. ___ Physical development including gross motor and/or fine motor skills
      c. ___ Communication
      d. ___ Social/emotional/affective development
      e. ___ Self-help skills
    2. ___ The student needs special education.

NOTE: If the developmental delay is the result of a vision and/or hearing loss, the student shall be determined eligible under either of those exceptionalities.

West Virginia Department of Education
March 2017

ELIGIBILITY DETERMINATION CHECKLIST

Student's Name: _____   **Date of EC Meeting** _____

F. Emotional/Behavioral Disorder - Documentation the student meets <u>ALL</u> of the following:
1. ___ The student continues to exhibit an emotional/behavioral disorder consistent with the definition after interventions have been implemented.
2. ___ The student has been observed exhibiting one or more of the characteristics listed in the definition of emotional/behavioral disorder and the characteristics have been documented:
   a. ___ For a long period of time; and
   b. ___ By more than one knowledgeable observer trained in data gathering; and
   c. ___ In more than one setting; and
   d. ___ At a level of frequency, duration, and/or intensity that is significantly different from the student's peers in the same or similar circumstances.
3. ___ The student's condition adversely affects educational performance in the area of academics, peer and/or teacher interaction, and/or participation in class/school activities.
4. ___ The student exhibits behavior(s) that is not primarily the result of physical, sensory or intellectual deficits.
5. ___ The student needs special education

G. Gifted (Grades One through Eight) - Documentation the student meets ALL of the following:
1. ___ General intellectual ability with a full scale score at the 97th percentile rank or higher on a comprehensive test of intellectual ability with consideration of 1.0 standard error of measurement;
2. ___ At least one of the four core curriculum areas of academic achievement at the 90th percentile rank or higher as measured by an individual standardized achievement test, or at least one of the four core curriculum areas of classroom performance demonstrating exceptional functioning as determined during the multidisciplinary evaluation; and
3. ___ The need for specially designed, differentiated instruction and/or services beyond those normally provided in the general classroom.

   NOTE: See Policy 2419 for Special Considerations

H. Exceptional Gifted (Grades Nine through Twelve) The eligibility criteria for gifted has been met. - Documentation the student meets one or more of the following:
1. ___ The eligibility criteria for one or more of the disabilities as defined in Policy 2419 and/or
2. ___ The definition for economically disadvantaged; and/or
3. ___ The definition for underachievement, which takes into consideration the student's ability level, educational performance and achievement levels; and/or
4. ___ The definition for psychological adjustment disorder as documented by a comprehensive psychological evaluation.

I. Hard of Hearing - Documentation the student meets <u>ALL</u> of the following:
1. ___ The student exhibits characteristics consistent with the definition and relies primarily on hearing to access spoken communication.
2. ___ The student has been diagnosed by an otologist, otolaryngologist, or audiologist as having a hearing loss.
3. ___ The student's condition adversely affects educational performance.
4. ___ The student needs special education.

J. Intellectual Disability - Documentation the student meets ALL of the following:
1. ___ Documentation will assure that the student meets one of the following:
   a. ___ The student with a mild to moderate intellectual disability has general intellectual functioning ranging from two to three standard deviations below the mean, in consideration of 1.0 standard error of measurement as determined by a qualified psychologist, using an individually administered intelligence test;
      OR
   b. ___ The student with the most significant cognitive disabilities(moderate to severe intellectual disability) has general intellectual functioning more than three standard deviations below the mean, in consideration of 1.0 standard error of measurement as determined by a qualified psychologist, using an individually administered intelligence test; AND
2. ___ The student exhibits concurrent deficits in adaptive functioning expected for his or her age across multiple environments based on clinical and standardized assessments in at least one of the following domains: conceptual, social or practical; and *
   a. ___ If intellectual functioning and adaptive functioning are inconsistent in severity*, an observation must be completed to determine the level of supports required.
      *See Appendix for Severity Levels for Adaptive Functioning.
      AND
3. ___ The age of onset is eighteen or below; AND
4. ___ The student's condition adversely affects educational performance; AND
5. ___ The student needs special education.

K. Orthopedic Impairment - Documentation the student meets <u>ALL</u> of the following:
1. ___ The student exhibits characteristics consistent with the definition.
2. ___ The student has an orthopedic impairment diagnosed and described by a licensed physician.
3. ___ The existence of educational needs as a result of the orthopedic impairment.
4. ___ The student's condition adversely affects educational performance.
5. ___ The student needs special education.

L. Other Health Impairment - Documentation the student meets <u>ALL</u> of the following:
1. ___ The student exhibits characteristics consistent with the definition;
2. ___ The student has a chronic or acute medical or health condition as diagnosed and described by a licensed physician; with the exception of ADHD which can be diagnosed by a school psychologist or licensed psychologist; and
3. ___ The existence of educational needs as a result of the medical or health condition.
4. ___ The student's condition adversely affects educational performance.
5. ___ The student needs special education.

M. Specific Learning Disability

The EC **MUST** complete the *Specific Learning Disability Team Report* form and attach the form to the *Eligibility Committee Report*.
West Virginia Department of Education
March 2017

ELIGIBILITY DETERMINATION CHECKLIST

Student's Name: _____   **Date of EC Meeting** _____

N. Speech/Language Impairment

Language – Documentation the student meets <u>ALL</u> the following:

1. ___ Two or more procedures, at least one of which yields a standard score, were used to assess both expressive and receptive modalities.
2. ___ **K-12:** Language abilities are substantially and quantifiably below those expected for the student's chronological age and cognitive state of development, resulting in functional limitation in effective communication, social participation, academic achievement or occupational performance individually or in any combination
    ___ **Preschool:** Language abilities had a negative impact on social-communicative interaction.
3. ___ Norm referenced language tests were administered which yield **two** subtest or total test scores with the following characteristics:
    a. ___ 1.5 or more standard deviations (SD) below the mean;
    b. ___ a language quotient/standard score of 78 (mean of 100);
    c. ___ a stanine of two and/or a percentile of 8; **AND/OR**
    d. ___ a non-standard/informal assessment indicates that the student has difficulty understanding and/or expressing ideas and/or concepts to such a degree that it interferes with the student's social/educational progress.
4. ___ The student's condition adversely affects educational performance.
5. ___ The student needs special education.

Speech Sound Disorder – Documentation the student meets <u>ALL</u> of the following:

1. ___ At least two procedures were used to assess the student, one of which is a standardized measure.
2. ___ Application of developmental norms from diagnostic tests verified that speech sounds may not develop without intervention.
3. ___ **K-12:** The student's speech has a negative impact on academic, social and/or vocational functioning, and one of the following characteristics exist:
    a. ___ Two or more of the phonemic errors not expected at the student's current age or developmental level were observed during direct testing;
    b. ___ Two or more of the phonological processes not expected at the student's current age or developmental level were observed during direct testing and/or conversational speech.
    ___ **Preschool:** The student's speech has a negative impact on social-communicative interactions and one of the following characteristics:
    a. ___ Multiple phonemic errors that significantly reduce the student's speech intelligibility and are not expected at the student's current age or developmental level were observed during direct testing and/or conversational speech;
    b. ___ Two or more phonological processes that significantly reduce the student's speech intelligibility and are not expected at the student's current age or developmental level were observed during direct testing and/or in conversational speech.
4. ___ The student's condition adversely affects educational performance.
5. ___ The student needs special education.

Childhood Onset Fluency Disorder (Stuttering) – Documentation the student meets <u>ALL</u> of the following:

1. ___ The student has a fluency rating of moderate or severe on the Suggested Guidelines for Stuttering Services or the Suggested Guidelines for Stuttering Services for Preschool.
2. ___ The student's condition adversely affects educational performance.
3. ___ The student needs special education.

Social (Pragmatic) Communication Disorder – Documentation the student meets <u>ALL</u> of the following:

1. ___ Assessment measures included norm referenced tests, multiple observations, checklists and structured tasks.
2. ___ Assessment procedures were used that were contextually based and involved multiple settings and communication partners.
3. ___ Assessment results indicated deficits in functional limitations in effective communication, social participation, social relationships, academic achievement and/or occupational performance, individually or in combination.
4. ___ Assessment results have eliminated the presence of restricted repetitive behaviors, interests and other activities related to the diagnosis of Autism.
5. ___ The student's condition adversely affects educational performance.
6. ___ The student needs special education.

Voice Disorder – Documentation the student meets <u>ALL</u> of the following:

1. ___ The student has a voice production rating of moderate or severe on the Voice Rating Scale.
2. ___ The existence or absence of a structural or functional pathology has been verified by an otolaryngologist.
3. ___ The student's condition adversely affects educational performance.
4. ___ The student needs special education.

Special Considerations – EC must respond to each of the following:

1. ___ Lack of discrepancy between cognitive level and communication performance was not the sole factor when determining eligibility for a severely speech and language disordered student.
2. ___ Eligibility for speech and language services was not determined on the basis of having a primary language other than English or a language difference.
3. ___ If verbal communication was not an effective means of communication for this student, an augmentative/alternative communication evaluation was conducted to determine the need for an alternative means of communication.

O. Traumatic Brain Injury - Documentation the student meets <u>ALL</u> of the following:

1. ___ The student has an acquired injury to the brain caused by an external physical force resulting in a total or partial functional disability or psychosocial impairment, or both as diagnosed by a licensed physician.
2. ___ The student's condition adversely affects educational performance.
3. ___ The student needs special education.

West Virginia Department of Education
March 2017

50   Stephen B. Richards

References

Frank, C. L., Christman, J. T., Baldwin, J. L., & Richards, S. B. (2019). *Managing classrooms and student behavior*. New York, NY: Routledge.

Smiley, L. R., Richards, S. B., & Taylor, R. L. (2019). *Exceptional students: Preparing teachers for the 21st Century* (3rd ed.). Columbus, OH: McGraw-Hill.

West Virginia Board of Education (2017). *Special Education Process Forms with Instructions*. Retrieved from www.wvde.us, 05/2020.

West Virginia Board of Education (2017). *Policy 2514 Regulations for Education of Exceptional Students (with revisions)*. Retrieved from www.wvde.us, 05/2020.

West Virginia Policy 2419: Regulations for the Education of Students with Exceptionalities (2017). Retrieved from wvde.state.wv.us, 07/2020.

4 Disabilities

Catherine Lawless Frank

Objectives: After reading this chapter, students will be able to:

1   Understand that a disability impacts a student's ability to learn and/
or participate in school
2   Identify the primary characteristics of each disability under IDEA
3   Recognize that educational needs are determined by the individual
rather than a list of disability characteristics.

Chapter 3 discussed the collaborative multi-factored evaluation process used to objectively examine a student's strengths and areas of need. The results of these assessments are summarized in a report (see Appendix A from Chapter 5) that is used by the multi-disciplinary team (also referred to as an Eligibility Committee) to determine whether a student meets the eligibility requirements for a specific disability. Each disability has specific identifying features that potentially impact a student's ability to learn and/or participate in school. When a student exhibits the characteristics associated with a disability, the school must then determine whether a student meets the requirements to the degree that special education services are necessary. For all disability categories under IDEA, the disability must:

1   have an adverse effect on educational performance, and
2   require special education services.

Chapter 3 provided an example of a student with a diagnosed condition that did not meet these two criteria.

Students with disabilities, aged 3–21, receiving special education services, make up about 14% (approximately 7 million students) of the public school population (National Center for Education Statistics, 2019). Each one of these 7 million students has their own unique sets of strengths and needs. The type of disability does not define the student but requires schools to develop programs and strategies to meet their *specific* educational needs. IDEA does not simply define a disability as a condition that hinders academic progress, but considers the student holistically and their ability to learn and participate in school. Special education, therefore, encompasses more than academics and may provide services for behavioral, functional, or adaptive living, social skills, and a variety of related services (such as speech and language, occupational or physical therapy, and mental health services). Some disabilities do directly impact academic or cognitive abilities (such as an Intellectual Disability) while others may have limited or no intellectual impact (such as a hearing or orthopedic impairment) but require an educational program to meet the students' unique needs.

This chapter will discuss the defining characteristics of each of the 13 categories of disability identified under IDEA, beginning with the most common or high-incidence disabilities. High-incidence disabilities include specific learning disabilities, intellectual disabilities, emotional disturbances and speech and language impairments. These are the more common disabilities accounting for approximately 80% *of students receiving special education services*. Autism (or more specifically Autism Spectrum Disorder) and other health impairments (which include attention deficit disorders with and without hyperactivity) encompass approximately 15% of students with disabilities. The seven remaining categories are considered low incidence, impacting roughly 5% of students with disabilities. All of the disabilities are defined through general characteristics that are present among students in that category. No student is likely to exhibit all characteristics and disabilities affect each person differently. A student's disability category only provides educators with a *very* general idea of what the student might be able to do or how they will perform in school.

These categories are most useful for schools and districts to report to state departments of education how many students receive special education services and in which categories. In turn, states report data to the U.S. Department of Education. This allows education and government agencies to have a better global understanding of what is occurring in special education. An example of why this is important is the fact that the number of students categorized as having autism is significantly higher in 2020 than in 1990 when autism first became an IDEA category. Educators and researchers in various fields (e.g., neuropsychology, medicine) have investigated why this increase occurred. In turn, educators and the public have come to learn that autism is a spectrum of disorders with wide-ranging effects in nature and severity. Another use of disability categories is to adjust school funding and to understand how the school-aged population of students with and without disabilities may be changing.

These statistics represent students whose IDEA category is their *primary* disability. Students may also have *secondary* disabilities. For example, students with the primary disability such as specific learning disabilities, intellectual disabilities, or emotional disturbances may also have a speech and language impairment as a secondary disability and also receive services to address it.

It is important to remember that a "specific learning disability" is only one of the 13 categories under IDEA. Those unfamiliar with special education may think that specific learning disability is a generic term that describes all students in special education when that is not the case. This distinction may not be particularly meaningful in actually *teaching* any specific student, but is nevertheless a distinction that is made in schools, districts, states, and by the federal government.

Specific Learning Disability

Specific learning disability is the largest disability category and consists of 34% of all special education students and 5% of the total school population (National Center for Education Statistics, 2019; National Center of Learning Disabilities, 2014). A specific learning disability (SLD) affects how a person understands, learns, and/or processes information. It typically involves written or spoken language (although mathematical processing may be impacted) and manifests as "the imperfect ability to listen, think, speak, read, write, spell, or do mathematical calculations" (20 U.S. C. § 1401 (30)). Most students with SLD have average to above-average intelligence but even with supports, struggle academically and/or achieve at a lower level than might be expected (e.g., perform at an average level when they are actually capable of performing at a higher level). These students have the ability to learn but a psychological processing issue inhibits their progress through conventional means. See Table 4.1 for Signs and Symptoms of SLD.

Specific learning disabilities are often viewed as a disability of exclusions. These students can learn but for some reason are not performing to their academic potential. To be identified as having an SLD requires all other potential inhibitory factors be eliminated as the primary cause of a student's learning concerns. Their challenges must not be "primarily the

Table 4.1 Signs and Symptoms of an SLD

Area	Signs and Symptoms
Reading difficulties	Difficulties with • phonemic awareness • phonological processing • decoding words • fluency • reading rate of reading • rhyming • spelling • vocabulary • reading comprehension • written expression.

(*continued*)

Table 4.1 (continued)

Area	Signs and Symptoms
Math	Difficulties with • counting • learning number facts • doing math calculations • measurement • telling time • counting money • estimating number quantities • mental math • problem-solving strategies.
Writing	• tight and awkward pencil grip and body position • tiring quickly while writing • trouble forming letter shapes • inconsistent spacing between letters or words • difficulty writing or drawing on a line or within margins • problems with syntax structure and grammar • a large gap between written ideas and understanding demonstrated through speech.
Auditory Processing	Difficulties with • auditory discrimination • auditory figure–ground discrimination • auditory memory • auditory sequencing • spelling, reading, and written expression.
Visual Processing	Difficulties with • visual discrimination • visual figure–ground discrimination • visual sequencing • visual motor processing • visual memory • visual closure • spatial relationships.
Executive Functioning	Difficulties in • planning • organizing • strategizing • remembering details • managing time and space efficiently.

Source: Cortiella & Horowitz, 2014.

result of visual, hearing, or motor disabilities, of intellectual disabilities, of emotional disturbance, or of environmental, cultural, or economic disadvantage" (20 U.S.C. § 1401 (30)). This means that the student's struggles cannot be caused by another disability or factors such as English as a second language, absenteeism, poverty, or mental health concerns. All other potential explanations are eliminated by the multidisciplinary evaluation team (MDET), leaving an SLD as the most likely reason for the student's learning problems. A student with a SLD may be an English language learner or live in poverty, but such variables do not serve to explain the student's learning problems.

SLD is identified through a severe discrepancy model focused on assessment scores, or a failure to respond to intervention or a combination of both approaches. The severe discrepancy model involves, in part, assessing the student's academic potential, often by use of IQ (intelligence quotient) testing and comparing IQ to actual academic achievement assessments.

For instance, if a student struggles with reading, SLD eligibility would be determined, in part, through individualized norm-referenced, standardized assessments of the student's IQ and reading knowledge and skills. The results of these assessments are then analyzed to determine whether a severe discrepancy exists between the student's potential or IQ and their actual academic achievement. For an SLD, IQ is typically in the average to the above-average range while their actual academic achievement is significantly lower than average. The severe discrepancy between IQ and actual achievement assessment scores is an indication of an SLD. The student can learn (average or above-average IQ) but is struggling to do so as indicated by significantly lower academic achievement scores. It is important to remember that these are not the only two assessments or criteria used in a multi-factored evaluation but a discrepancy between these two assessment scores can be indicative of an SLD. Also, not all states use IQ tests and may use other assessments to determine learning potential.

The severe discrepancy method has been in use since IDEA was implemented. It can be, in a very real sense, a "numbers game" because identification of SLD may rely on mathematical calculations to determine whether the discrepancy between potential and actual achievement standard scores is significantly large. The calculation may rely on the magnitude in the difference between potential and achievement expressed in standard deviations. For example, a student might have an IQ score of 100 (exactly average) and have a reading achievement score of 80 which is below average. The discrepancy between the two scores would be 1.33 standard deviations. While the student may indeed be struggling, if the severe discrepancy model being used requires a difference of at least 1.5 or even 2.0 standard deviations, the student may not "qualify" as needing special education services.

This method has also been referred to as a "wait to fail" model. In other words, a student may be exhibiting learning difficulties for some period of time (e.g., in 1st and 2nd grades) *before* the assessment scores reach the severe discrepancy level at the 3rd grade. Because of this serious issue of delaying individual interventions to help the student, the response to intervention method is now strongly recommended as a replacement of or a complement to the severe discrepancy method. The severe discrepancy method by itself is not considered best practice in assessing students for eligibility for SLD.

In the RTI approach, the school uses a multi-tiered system of support (discussed in Chapter 2) to mitigate academic and behavioral concerns. If a student fails to make adequate progress even after receiving increasingly focused instruction, it may be an indication of an SLD. In this approach, the school implements and exhausts their repertoire of Tier 2 interventions without the expected gains in achievement or learning, and the student continues to struggle. The school then may determine, through the MFE/MDET process, that the student's failure to respond to interventions is most likely due to an SLD.

A tremendous advantage of the RTI method is that data are gathered in actual teaching and learning situations in the natural classroom environment and in response to increasingly individualized and intensive interventions. The severe discrepancy model may be over-reliant on scores on tests that are administered outside of the classroom and represent the student's performance only on the particular days of testing.

Neither the severe discrepancy method nor the failure to respond to interventions approach is *mandated* by IDEA and many districts use a combination of both approaches. Schools implement a support framework, such as RTI, to identify areas of concern, provide increasing levels of interventions, and monitor progress consistently. If the student fails to make adequate progress even with increasing levels of intervention, then assessments are administered to determine whether a discrepancy exists between expected levels of performance (IQ) and academic achievement. If the student fails to respond to interventions and exhibits a discrepancy between IQ and achievement, then they might be determined to have an SLD. Using this combination of methods, there may be no specific numerical discrepancy (e.g., 1.5 standard deviation difference) required between the assessment scores. The standardized assessment scores are a complement to the data gathered through the RTI process. It is important to remember that all other physical, environmental, and psychological disorders and factors must be eliminated as the primary cause before a student can be identified as SLD. The MTSS approach can also be much more useful in eliminating other factors through addressing those factors along with the learning interventions during the RTI process (e.g., providing nutritional support, counseling, social services, etc.).

Case Study 4.1 Determining Eligibility for SLD

Since she began attending school, Saida has struggled with language arts. In Kindergarten, she lagged behind her peers in identifying letters, letter–sound correspondence, and writing her first name. Through the universal screen process in the fall, she was identified as a student of concern, and her progress in language arts was monitored on a biweekly basis. An analysis of her data in early winter indicated she continued to lag behind her peers and did not make adequate progress. The school decided to begin providing her additional small-group language arts instruction weekly for 30 minutes. While Saida was improving, her growth rate trailed behind that of her peers, and the achievement gap between them continued to grow.

In 1st and 2nd grades, Saida's teachers reported that she was quiet, shy, and, at times, slow to follow directions and begin assignments. Saida rarely asked questions or sought help even when she was confused. Her teachers tried various accommodations and continued providing small-group language arts intervention twice a week, but data indicated she was only making minimal progress. Saida's failure to respond to intervention led the school to suspect she may have a Severe Learning Disability (SLD). At the beginning of 3rd grade, she was referred for special education assessment.

The school decided to use the assessment discrepancy method and the failure to respond to intervention as the basis for determining eligibility. Documentations of Saida's inability to respond to interventions beginning in Kindergarten were included in her school records. She was then assessed using the Weschler Intelligence Scale for Children (WISC III) as part of the assessment discrepancy method to determine her IQ and the Weschler Individual Achievement Test (WIAT) to evaluate her academic achievement in critical areas.

The WISC III determined Saida had average IQ (average is between 85 and 115) with an overall or Full-Scale IQ of 98. She received the following results:

WISC III

Performance IQ 107
Verbal IQ 89
Full-Scale IQ 98

On the WIAT, Saida received a range of scores that indicated areas of strengths and needs (average scores again are between 85 and 115). Her results showed the following scores:

WIAT

Basic Reading 67
Mathematic Reasoning 99
Spelling 77
Reading Comprehension 72
Numerical Operations 101
Listening Comprehension 86
Oral Expression 91

Saida earned average scores (as would be expected based on her IQ) on the WIAT in Mathematic Reasoning (99), Numeral Operations (101), and Oral Expression (91), indicating her achievement is at or near her expected levels in those academic areas. She earned scores considerably lower and below expectations based on her IQ in Basic Reading (67), Spelling (77), Reading Comprehension (72), and Listening Comprehension (86).

The results of both assessments indicated that Saida had an average IQ and academic strengths in Mathematics (reasoning and number operations) but was achieving below expected levels in language arts (basic reading, spelling, reading comprehension). These results indicated a discrepancy between her IQ and achievement levels in language arts. This discrepancy and her failure to respond to intervention suggested that Saida had an SLD. The eligibility assessment process also eliminated other potential causes for her language arts challenges, including deficits in hearing and vision, and environmental, cultural, or economic disadvantages. Using both failure to respond to intervention and the assessment discrepancy method, while eliminating all other potential causes, the school, in collaboration with Saida's parents, determined that she had a Severe Learning Disability and was eligible for special education services.

SLD is not a disease or illness that can be cured, but is a challenge that impacts many facets of a person's life. In fact, the actual cause of a student's SLD is seldom identifiable as opposed to a condition such as Down syndrome. Approximately 80% of people with SLD experience lifelong difficulties with reading, but the impact is not limited to language arts classes. SLD can also impact psychological processes such as perception, attention, memory, metacognition, and organization, and nonacademic areas such as social skills and motor coordination (Texas Council for Developmental Disabilities, 2013d). No two people with SLD have the same characteristics and it is essential to provide the individualized skills and supports necessary for success. While these supports should include academic areas, it is equally important to assist in developing organizational, metacognition, memory, and social skills. These types of supports are discussed in greater detail in Chapter 8.

Specific teaching strategies for SLD

- Chunk or break larger assignments or concepts into smaller components or steps
- Provide clear, specific feedback on what students are doing right and wrong

- Use clear specific language, visual supports, and organizers such as graphic organizers, diagrams, manipulatives, and pictures
- Teach learning strategies, memorization, and organizational skills and have students reflect on their impact and where the strategy can be applied
- Implement direct instruction (such as "I do, we do, you do") and connect lessons to prior and future learning and provide real-life applications (Learning Disabilities Association of America, 2013).

Direct instruction is explained in greater detail in Chapter 7. One final note, some educators may use the term LD (learning disability) rather than SLD.

Intellectual Disabilities

Individuals with intellectual disability (ID) can function quite capably in many environments, such as social and vocational situations, but struggle academically and intellectually. These students learn at a slower pace and often face challenges with memorizing and recalling information as well as transferring and generalizing information to new environments. An ID impacts basic academic skills (such as reading, writing, and mathematics) and adaptive living skills (such as communication, social skills, independent living skills, and personal care). Students can and do learn academic and adaptive skills, but not usually at the level or pace as students without ID. Activities that require self-determination, choice making, problem solving and goal setting are also often challenging for people with ID and typically the achievement gap between their performance and that of their typically developing peers widens with age (Texas Council for Developmental Disabilities, 2013c). This gap grows as the demands of school and life (e.g., from elementary to middle to high school to adulthood) increase and become more complex. For example, learning to add single or double-digit numbers may well be within the zone of proximal development for a student with ID during the elementary years. But, the same student is much less likely to perform 3-digit long division, trigonometry, or algebra skills as they progress through school.

ID consists of approximately 6% of students receiving special education services with 17% spending most of their school day in a general education classroom (National Center for Education Statistics, 2019). As discussed in the previous paragraph, inclusion in general education classes may diminish over time as the achievement gap grows. General education teachers at the elementary level are likely to have one or more students with ID included in their classes. Conversely, high school teachers may have few or no students with ID included in their content area classes. So, the percentage of students with ID who spend most of their day in general education will change as you move up in grade levels.

Eligibility is determined in part through assessments that determine three important aspects of the IDEA definition including:

1   a significantly below-average IQ (typically below 70–75 with an average IQ being 85–115) and
2   deficits in adaptive concepts such as time, language, and literacy, social skills (e.g., interpersonal skills, gullibility, and problem solving), and practical skills (e.g., daily living, health care, and financial awareness) that are used in everyday life, and
3   these issues must be evident during the developmental period (birth–18 years of age).

IDs are developmental disabilities. In other words, students with milder ID in particular may have had the biological capacity to achieve at typical levels at school age. Variables such as lack of language and cognitive stimulation in early childhood, malnutrition, poor health care, homelessness, and so on can take their toll on children over time such that at school age they are much less well "equipped" to learn and thrive in academic environments.

In general, the public may think of ID as including those with biological issues such as Down Syndrome or Fragile X syndrome when, in fact, there may be no such directly identifiable cause of the ID. ID may range from milder to quite severe as to how it impacts a student's overall ability to learn and adapt to present and future environments. Those with more severe ID tend to be those who have conditions identified in early life (e.g., genetic syndromes). Most students in this category have milder ID and do not necessarily appear different from their peers without disabilities until they are required to engage in more advanced developmental skills, academic skills, more complex social skills, and more demanding life skills as school begins and continues.

Teachers need to build on the strengths of students with ID while promoting independence and self-reliance. Initially, teachers should assume a student can learn academic and other skills until repeated opportunities reveal whatever limitations exist. The student's limitations may become clearer through an RTI process. Direct instructional strategies used to teach functional skills (such as money, time, independent living, personal care, and hygiene) and vocational skills can help students develop the adaptive abilities necessary to lead independent and fulfilling lives. Since transferring and generalizing skills is often a challenge, it is beneficial to teach skills using authentic materials (such as using real money instead of fake money) in the natural environment (school or community) (Texas Council for Developmental Disabilities, 2013c). Transfer of skills means a student learns a skill in one environment (e.g., learning to count in a resource room) and applies it in another (e.g., counting in the 1st grade classroom). Generalization occurs when a student can take a skill and use it in new environments and in novel ways. For example, a student may learn the four times multiplication facts (4 x 1 = 4, 4 x 2 = 8, and so on). The student then generalizes the same skill to figure out the cost of four $1.00 candy bars at the neighborhood convenience store.

Specific strategies for ID

- Incorporate student's strengths and interests into lessons to make learning achievable and relevant
- Break down larger tasks, assignments, and activities into small steps and teach the individual steps in chronological order
- Provide multiple opportunities to practice skills in a variety of different settings
- Use physical, visual, and verbal prompting to scaffold and support learning
- Focus on both academic and adaptive living skills to promote independence and self-determination in present and future environments.

Emotional Disturbance

Students who are considered emotionally disturbed (ED) have behaviors that interfere with their ability to learn and/or participate in school and constitute approximately 5% of those receiving special education services (National Center for Education Statistics, 2019). The qualifying conditions for ED are somewhat broad and can be found in Table 4.2. These conditions generally result in the factors that constitute ED and typically point to inappropriate behavior or emotional response in normal situations and circumstances. These behaviors can be externalizing (such as physical or verbal aggression, refusal to follow directions or rules, and difficulty regulating behaviors) or internalizing (such as depression, anxiety, and withdrawal). Whether a student has an externalizing or internalizing issues, the condition often impacts relationships with peers and/or adults. Students with ED have difficulties learning that are not associated with an intellectual or sensory disability. ED includes mental health disorders such as anxiety, bipolar, conduct, and psychotic disorders. There is also a strong correlation to communication issues for students with ED with approximately 71% having deficits in expressive and/or receptive language (Texas Council for Developmental Disabilities, 2013b).

It is important to note that a disproportional number of African Americans, males, and students from lower socioeconomic status are identified as being ED. The eligibility characteristics in this disability are more subjective with no specific medical criteria or assessment scores necessary. The terminology used, such as "to a marked degree," "over a long period of time," and "socially maladjusted" (see Table 4.2) are not clearly defined and are open to interpretation as is the impact of the behaviors on the student's ability to learn and/or participate in school. This ambiguity potentially

Table 4.2 IDEA Definition of Emotionally Disturbed

a condition exhibiting one or more of the following characteristics over a long period of time and to a marked degree that adversely affects a child's educational performance:

    A. An inability to learn that cannot be explained by intellectual, sensory, or health factors;

    B. An inability to build or maintain satisfactory interpersonal relationships with peers and teachers;

    C. Inappropriate types of behavior or feelings under normal circumstances;

    D. A general pervasive mood of unhappiness or depression; or

    E. A tendency to develop physical symptoms or fears associated with personal or school problems. The term includes schizophrenia.

The term does not apply to children who are socially maladjusted, unless it is determined that they have an emotional disturbance (ED).

allows for bias in the identification process, which must be addressed in culturally responsive ways when determining eligibility (Richards, Lawless Frank, Sableski & Arnold, 2016; Texas Council for Developmental Disabilities, 2013c). With some students (e.g., depression/anxiety disorders, childhood schizophrenia, bipolar disorder), their conditions are psychologically or medically diagnosed by non-school professionals which largely determine eligibility. Many students in this category exhibit "acting out" behaviors or non-compliance that might also be diagnosed by psychological or medical professions. However, school personnel may also be identifying students aside from or in addition to these more formal diagnoses.

While the dominating characteristic of this disability is inappropriate behavior, it is equally important to address academic needs. While students with ED have a wide range of intellectual abilities, they are more likely to drop out of school, struggle academically, function below grade level and encounter greater challenges in math and spelling (Texas Council for Developmental Disabilities, 2013c). Providing the support necessary for the student to be successful academically can help mitigate behavioral concerns and build the foundation for an appropriate quality relationship between the teacher and student. Developing an appropriate relationship in which the student feels cared for and supported is critical to addressing both academic and behavioral needs.

Case Study 4.2 Application ED

Read the following student scenarios and complete the discussion questions.

Most of the time, Robert behaves like a typical student. He gets along well with teachers and peers and usually is a pleasure to have in class. Sometimes, though, while seated at his desk, Robert withdraws into himself, becomes despondent, and cries. His teachers report that this behavior occurred three times in the last two weeks but only twice last year. The increased frequency of these episodes is beginning to impact his relationships with peers. His teachers have been supportive but are worried about his mental health. Robert lives with his father, two brothers, and several other cousins and uncles. His father is supportive, involved, and aware of Robert's behaviors. He attributes Robert's episodes to missing his mom, who he has not seen since he was three years old, and lack of sleep due to the large number of people living in the house.

Jeremy is disruptive and appears to have difficulty following directions, especially in language arts class. In a 45-minute classroom observation in language arts, he did not follow the teacher's verbal instructions three times ("put away your phone," "stop leaning back in your chair," and "face the front of the room"). It took him over two minutes to follow seven verbal directions ("sit down" twice, "be quiet" three times, "take out your textbook," and "stop bothering your classmates"). On average, it took his classmates less than 25 seconds to follow the teacher's directions. Jeremy also appeared off-task (playing with objects, talking to peers, not following, along with reading in class) for approximately 23 minutes during the 45-minute class period. He disrupted class five times (yelling out answers/questions/comments, threw a paper wad at a peer). In contrast, in a 45-minute observation in math class, Jeremy followed the teacher's directions all but one time ("keep all four legs of your chair on the floor") and took over two minutes to follow one teacher direction ("please take out your math books"). He appeared off-task for approximately five minutes (playing with an object at his desk) but completed his assignment within the allotted class period. His math class behavior was similar to that of his peers, except for the amount of time it took for him to take out his math book.

Sally has an average IQ but struggles academically and appears to have few if any friends. Her difficulties with social skills often make her seem "strange" or "rude" to her peers. On average, she visits the school nurse three times per week, mainly due to stomach complaints. In class, she is typically quiet and withdrawn, but, at times, appears to be rocking back and forth and murmuring to herself. She rarely asks or answers questions, contributes to class discussions, or completes assignments in class but does complete some homework. She lives with her mother, who works two low wage jobs and is often home alone. Due to her work schedule, the school has had limited contact with the mother.

Discussion Questions:

1   Which components of IDEA eligibility definition for Emotionally Disturbed (see Table 4.2) does each of the three students (Jeremy, Robert, and Sally) exhibit?

> 2   In your opinion, do any of the students appear to exhibit behaviors to a "marked degree"?
> 3   What additional information is necessary to determine whether each of the three students has ED? Would help in the discussion making process?

Specific strategies for ED

- Determine the cause or trigger of a student's behavior and teach more appropriate replacement strategies
- Provide positive feedback at a significantly greater rate than negative feedback (for instances, a minimum of five positive statements on what the student is doing correctly for every one negative statement about what the student is doing wrong)
- Use clear specific language in lessons and directions
- Allow wait time (up to 7 seconds) when asking a question or providing directions
- Supply the necessary instructional supports to limit frustration and complete the task.

A final note, some educators and states may use terms such as serious emotional disturbance or emotional/behavioral disorder for this category.

Speech and Language Impairment

A speech and language impairment (SLI) is a communication disorder that adversely affects speech skills, language skills, or both. Speech disorders include:

1   Articulation disorders include substitutions (such as "wabbit" for "rabbit"), omissions (such as "un" for "sun"), and additions (such as "boyee" for "boy").
2   Fluency disorders (primarily stuttering), and
3   Voice disorders (raspy, hoarse, too low pitched, too high pitched – voice disorders are relatively rare in children) (Center for Parent Information and Resources, 2015).

Language disorders include a number of different specific issues but can be broken down into three broad types:

1   Expressive language disorders that affect the abilities to express oneself orally or in writing
2   Receptive language disorders that affect the abilities to understand spoken communication and read for comprehension, and

3 Some educators also include pragmatic disorders that affect the ability to engage in social interaction (particularly conversations) that are satisfactory to both speaker and listener (an individual engaged in a conversation provides one-word answers to questions and does not engage in asking reciprocal questions). For example, Where are you from originally? "New York." Do you like it here? "Okay." Do you play any sports? "Baseball." I like baseball, what position do you play? "Outfield." The conversation is not likely to continue for very long nor lead to any genuine social connection to the person asking questions.

SLIs are typically diagnosed by a speech and language pathologist (SLP) and affect 19% of students receiving special education services making it the second-largest disability category behind SLD (National Center for Education Statistics, 2019). As previously stated, students who have a different primary disability may also exhibit a secondary SLI. Students whose primary disability is SLI comprise less than 19%. Again, it is important to understand, a student could have a speech disorder only, language disorder only, or both.

There is no direct correlation between cognitive ability and an SLI, but its impact on communication can affect many aspects of a student's academic and social life. Impaired ability to communicate can influence personal relationships, listening comprehension, reading fluency and comprehension, oral and written expression, socialization, and classroom participation. While SLI services can be directly provided by an SLP, teachers can support the SLP's work and incorporate a student's speech and language objectives into the classroom. General and special education teachers may find their interactions with SLPs are through consultation as much or more often than direct services provided to the student. Teachers need to be sensitive to the overarching impact of SLI and provide a supportive environment that fosters both academic and social growth.

Specific strategies for SLI

- Foster a positive social environment in the classroom and be sensitive to the student's receptive and expressive issues (e.g., asking a student who stutters to speak or read in front of the class when the student is uncomfortable)
- Collaborate with the speech and language pathologist to integrate services into the classroom
- Incorporate supports for listening, speaking, reading, writing, and communication development such as vocabulary acquisition, concept development, and use of academic terms and language
- Provide wait time for students to comprehend and process information and directions
- Provide ample opportunities for students to practice their communication skills in both academic and social circumstances.

Comprehension check

1   Identify the characteristics of an SLD.
2   What are the three main components of an ID?
3   Why is it important to be aware of the subjectivity of an ED diagnosis?
4   What is a difference between an expressive and receptive language impairment?

Autism

Autism or Autism Spectrum Disorder (ASD) is a neurological disorder that impacts approximately 1 in 59 children or 10% of students receiving services for special education. Males are diagnosed with ASD four times more often than females (1 in 37 males versus 1 in 151 females) but the gap between genders is narrowing (Center for Disease Control and Prevention, 2018; National Center for Education Statistics, 2019). Before 2013, autism was defined as a pervasive developmental disability with five subcategories (Autism, Asperger's Disorder, Childhood Disintegrative Disorder, Rett's Disorder, and Pervasive Developmental Disorder–Not Otherwise Specified). In 2013, four of the subcategories (Rett's Disorder was not included) were merged and became Autism Spectrum Disorder (ASD). ASD affects a person's behavior (repetitive or fixated patterns of behavior), socialization (difficulties interacting with others and developing relationships), and communication (struggles with speech or language disorders or both) (Texas Council for Developmental Disabilities, 2013a).

Since ASD is a spectrum disorder, its affects on behavior, communication, and socialization cause varying degrees of impacts, strengths, and challenges in individuals. About 40% of people with ASD have average to above average intelligence, whereas approximately 25% are nonverbal and exhibit characteristics associated with intellectual disabilities. While most desire to be included socially, people with ASD often struggle to engage in conversations, may fixate on a single topic, and have difficulties with eye contact and personal space. They often find challenges in new situations or environments. They may not use appropriate pragmatic or social skills and may engage in repetitive, self-stimulating behaviors (for instance, rocking back and forth or flapping hands) (What Is Autism?, 2015). People with ASD also have many strengths and positive attributes. Their fixation on topics can lead to a greater understanding of the details involved and mastery of a concept (e.g., considerable depth of knowledge of dinosaurs, math skills well beyond their same-age peers). They tend to be honest, non-judgmental, and have strong visual and memory skills. Building on their strengths is important to engaging them in the classroom and to fostering the necessary behavioral, social, and communication skills for success in school and the community.

Specific teaching strategies for ASD

- Use clear, specific language (avoid jargon, slang) and short, simple sentences and directions
- Implement visual support and picture cues to clarify key ideas, directions, and concepts
- Establish a consistent classroom routine and structure and communicate (orally and with picture cues); prepare students for changes in the classroom routine (e.g., a school assembly, working on math prior to English Language Arts (ELA) when it is usually the reverse)
- Provide cues for transition times (e.g., "Finish up what you are doing. We are leaving for lunch in 5 minutes.")
- Focus on the students' strengths and incorporate their interests into daily lessons
- Take opportunities to teach students social skills (e.g., "You took her scissors from her box. What should you have done first?"). Remember, teaching social skills should be conducted positively and not negatively (e.g., "You took her scissors without asking! Give them back right now!").

A final note is there is no compelling medical or scientific evidence through controlled studies indicating ASD is the direct result of vaccination.

Other Health Impaired

Other Health Impaired or OHI is an overarching category that encompasses physical and neurological disabilities not otherwise specified in IDEA. Many different conditions may fall under OHI including asthma, Type I diabetes, sickle cell anemia, cystic fibrosis, leukemia, attention deficit disorders. OHIs may negatively impact a person's ability to learn and/ or participate in school. There is not a single set of requirements, learning ability or medical condition for eligibility under OHI but identification for educational purposes is based on the impact of a disability on a student's ability to learn and participate in school. Generally, conditions are medically diagnosed and then an MDET determines the condition has an adverse impact on educational performance and requires special education.

The largest number of students serviced under OHI have attention deficit disorder (ADD) or attention deficit hyperactivity disorder (ADHD). Both are medical conditions that impact a person's ability to focus and attend and, in the case of ADHD, control behavior. Since neither ADD nor ADHD are disability categories under IDEA, determining eligibility for services is based on the unique characteristics and educational impact of the disability on a student. Depending on its severity, a student with ADD or ADHD may receive special education services under IDEA, accommodations through a 504 plan or receive no additional services at all.

Similarly, one student could have asthma that does not adversely impact educational performance and therefore, does not require special education services. Another student may have a 504 plan to address any issues that occasionally arise in school. A third student may have such severe asthma that they are medicated, suffer effects on a daily basis, miss school frequently, and be served under an IEP.

Specific teaching strategies for OHI

- Collaborate and communicate with families and other school professionals to address the unique needs of the student (as needed, be aware of health/medical issues)
- Provide specific structure and routines in the classroom but maintain flexibility for students whose disabilities affect them on varying days or times
- Ensure the classroom's physical layout and instructional activities accommodate the needs of the student
- Allow for accommodations, snack and break times, and time to attend to any medical needs as necessary for the student's disability
- Reduce distractions and highlight key information
- Plan means for "catching up" students who may miss school.

Students with OHI may receive more related services and accommodations than direct services through a special education teacher. The student with asthma receiving special education services may need occasional checks and medication administered by a school nurse, special accommodations in physical education, and limitations on outside activities during allergy season. The student may only receive services from the special education teacher after missing multiple days of school and has a need to receive individual help to catch up with peers.

IDEA include seven additional disability categories that, combined, make up approximately 5% of students receiving special education services (National Center for Education Statistics, 2019), and only fractions of a percent of the overall student population. While these disabilities are smaller in actual student numbers, they are typically aligned to specific medical or educational needs with a wide range of cognitive, physical, behavioral, and functional impacts. Many teachers may never encounter students with these conditions and, therefore, the discussion will be limited accordingly.

Four of the remaining disabilities involve hearing and/or vision loss and include deafness, hearing impairments, visual impairments, and deaf-blindness. In each of these disability categories, there exist "medical" diagnoses that are used to determine various agency and adult services. These medical diagnoses, however, do not always reveal how the student may perform in school. For each student under IDEA, the condition must have (1) an adverse impact on educational performance and (2) require special education services. MDETs make the determinations as a rule for these two criteria. The following discussions are adapted from Smiley, Richards, and Taylor (2019).

Deafness is medically defined by a severe to profound hearing loss diagnosed by an "ear, nose, throat" physician and audiologist. Medical diagnosis of deafness is determined by hearing loss based on the loudness that sounds must be to be heard (decibels) and by pitch/frequency (hertz). Educationally, a student may be considered deaf if they are unable to use their hearing for learning. Such a student will need emphasis on visual learning and/or may need sign language accommodations such as an interpreter or even a special education class for deaf students.

Hearing impairment (often referred to as hard of hearing) is diagnosed usually as having a moderate to severe hearing loss. Pitch can be particularly important because hearing losses can differ in this regard. Important in school is whether a student has perception and understanding of human speech. Amplification (hearing aids, FM/loop systems) are generally helpful for students who are hard of hearing. These students may need accommodations (e.g., preferential seating, more visual cues) and related services (e.g., speech and language and audiological services) more than direct special education services. Students who are hard of hearing from an educational perspective can still learn through spoken language and hearing. Finally, students can experience deafness in one ear and be hard of hearing in the other. Again, it is the effect on education and how the student best learns that is important for teachers. Functional hearing assessments by a specialist can be quite helpful in determining how well the student can use their hearing, whether there is assistive technology that can help, and what are effective teaching methods/materials.

Students who are **visually impaired** are classified in school as blind or low vision (sometimes referred to as partially sighted). Again, these are diagnoses made by medical physicians based on variables such as acuity (sharpness of vision at different distances), field of vision (e.g., the student has limited peripheral vision or "blind spots"), or ocular motility issues (e.g., continuous rapid movements of the eyes, eyes that are not aligned). For educators, the distinction between blindness and low vision is whether the student can use their vision effectively to learn with accommodations even when using corrective lenses. A student who is considered blind may have some vision, but is not able to read or write without soft- and hardware accommodations such as text to speech and speech to text. These students may need learning materials to be more auditory and tactile.

Similarly, a student who is low vision can use their vision to learn but may need accommodations such as large print books/materials or audio textbooks, but still use vision very much to learn. A functional vision assessment by a specialist can be very helpful in determining how well a student uses their vision, the most useful assistive technology, and teaching methods/materials.

Deaf–blindness means a student has a significant degree of both hearing and vision loss such that accommodations and services for students who are deaf/hard of hearing or blind/low vision are not sufficient by themselves so that a combination of approaches is needed. Students need not be medically deaf or blind to be eligible. These students may need much in the way of special education services, as conditions that lead to both hearing and vision loss may also affect cognitive and physical functioning. However, it would wrong for any teacher to assume that a student identified as having deaf–blindness is significantly affected other than by the sensory impairments themselves. This is a very low incidence disability and most general or special education teachers will not teach students with deaf–blindness on any sort of regular basis.

The remaining three categories are the results of medical conditions, injury to the brain, and/or having more than one significant disability. They include orthopedic impairments, traumatic brain injury, and multiple disabilities and each has a differing impact on how a student learns and participates in school.

An **orthopedic impairment** (OI) is a physical disability that limits mobility, dexterity, and/or stamina and results from an impairment (such as spina bifida or cerebral palsy), disease (such as muscular dystrophy) or musculoskeletal disorder (such as rheumatoid arthritis or limb deficiency). Some conditions affect health and physical abilities such as cerebral palsy and muscular dystrophy. Orthopedic impairments are medically diagnosed with the MDET establishing the adverse effect on educational performance and the need for special education services. This category, similar to OHI, includes many possible conditions with a wide range of impacts on learning and participation in school. The accommodations and instructional needs of students with OI are individually determined because there are so many conditions included in the category. Even with individual conditions such as cerebral palsy, the overall impacts can vary substantially from one student to the next. Many of the same strategies and materials used with OHI students can be used with students with OI as well. OI students may also need considerable related services such as physical and occupational therapy, special transportation, assistive technology, and so on.

A **traumatic brain injury** (TBI) is an acquired injury or damage to the brain by an external force occurring after birth that alters how the brain functions. TBIs can be open (the skull is actually penetrated) or closed (no penetration such as with a concussion). TBI in school-aged individuals may be the result of sports injuries, vehicle, and other types of accidents. It differs from other conditions in that the damage occurs after birth and is not the result of any medical or biological disease or condition. The injury may range from mild to severe and can have many different impacts on thinking, learning, psychological health, speech, language, motor skills, and so on. When a student has a severe TBI, they may be in a medical rehabilitation facility for some time before transitioning back to school. It is impossible to know how a student will be affected in school simply by a label of TBI. Strategies and accommodations associated with SLD, ID, and virtually all other disability categories may be applicable to any given student with TBI. It is important for teachers to understand that with TBI, the knowledge and skills acquired by a student prior to the injury may or may not be retained, may be altered, or may take time to be restored partially or fully. In other words, students with TBI may change over time as the brain works to overcome the damage from the injury.

Multiple disabilities (MD) refers to a student with two or more significant disabilities (such as ID and visual impairment or autism and OI) that cannot be accommodated in a program designed for a single disability. Not all, but a number of students with MDs do have intellectual disabilities. Again, the diagnoses are medical in nature. How best to educate a student with an MD will draw upon the strategies and accommodations for the individual disabilities as well as the combinations and include a full array of special education and related services.

Some schools and districts include **developmental delay** (DD) as a fourteenth category for special education but it is not mandatory to do so under IDEA. This category is designed for children aged three to nine or a subset thereof (for instance three- to five-year-olds), with delays in physical, cognitive, communication, social and/or emotional, or adaptive development. If the delay is temporary and the child overcomes the deficit, then they will no longer require special education services. If the delay is not remediated, then the child may eventually receive services under one of the other 13 disability categories. The purpose of including DD, as suggested, is typically to allow students who are lagging behind their peers developmentally to catch up, and avoid unnecessarily labeling a child who may have entered the school system with delays that might be remediated.

Comprehension Check

1 What are the three main aspects of an ASD?
2 Which population of students with disabilities is covered under OHI?
3 Why are some disabilities considered low incidence?

IDEA mandates that students with disabilities be educated in their least restrictive environment or alongside their general education peers to the maximum extent appropriate. This means that the vast majority of students with disabilities spend at least part if not all of their time in the general education classroom using the same curriculum as their general education peers. This makes it important for teachers to be knowledgeable about the general characteristics of each disability, to meet the needs of all students including those with disabilities. However, the most important characteristic a teacher can acquire is an open mind about what a student can achieve. Forming a collaborative team of educators to support one another, as well as students, is critical. Being a professional means accepting challenges and helping each and every student learn and grow. Chapters 6–8 include more on approaches to educating students with disabilities through a collaborative effort. Chapter 5 will include the content and development of IEPs that specify the special education services a student needs.

References

Center for Disease Control and Prevention (2018). Prevalence of autism spectrum disorder among children aged 8 years: Autism and developmental disabilities monitoring network, 11 sites, United States, 2014. *Surveillance Summaries*, April 27, 2018, 67(6), 1–23.

Center for Parent Information and Resources (2015). *Speech and language impairments*. Retrieved from www.parentcenterhub.org/speechlanguage/.

Cortiella, C., & Horowitz, S. H. (2014). *The state of learning disabilities* (3rd ed.). New York, NY: National Center of Learning Disabilities.

Individuals with Disabilities Education Act, 20 U.S.C. § 1400 (2004).

Learning Disabilities Association of America (2013, October 15). Successful strategies for teaching students with learning disabilities. Retrieved from https://ldaamerica.org/successful-strategies-for-teaching-students-with-learning-disabilities/.

National Center for Education Statistics (2019). Children and youth with disabilities. Retrieved from https://nces.ed.gov/programs/coe/indicator_cgg.asp.

Richards, S., Lawless Frank, C., Sableski, M., & Arnold, J. (2016). *Collaboration among professional, students, families and communities*. New York, NY: Routledge.

Smiley, L. R., Richards, S. B., & Taylor, R. L. (2019). *Exceptional students: Preparing teachers for the 21st century* (3rd ed.). Columbus, OH: McGraw-Hill.

Texas Council for Developmental Disabilities. (2013a). Autism. Austin, TX. Retrieved from www.projectidealonline.org/v/autism/.

Texas Council for Developmental Disabilities. (2013b). Emotional disturbance. Austin, TX. Retrieved from www.projectidealonline.org/v/emotional-disturbance/.

Texas Council for Developmental Disabilities. (2013c). Intellectual Disabilities. Austin, TX. Retrieved from www.projectidealonline.org/v/intellectual-disabilities/.

Texas Council for Developmental Disabilities. (2013d). Specific learning disabilities. Austin, TX. Retrieved from www.projectidealonline.org/v/specific-learning-disabilities/.

What is autism? (2015). Retrieved from www.projectidealonline.org/v/autism/, 07/13/2015.

5 Individualized Education Programs

Stephen B. Richards and Sarah Schimmel

Objectives: After reading the chapter, students will be able to:

1 Identify the required steps prior to the implementation of an Individualized Education Program (IEP)
2 Identify the components of an IEP
3 Identify the role of general and special education teachers in the writing and implementation of an IEP.

Chapter 1 included the principles associated with IDEA (e.g., FAPE, nondiscriminatory evaluation, parental participation, IEP, LRE, due process procedures) and other laws affecting the provision of general and special education services. In Chapter 2, we reviewed the RTI process within an MTSS used in identifying students who are at-risk for inadequate educational progress. Chapter 3 reviewed how at-risk students may be assessed and identified for special education services. In Chapter 4, the disability categories and definitions for which students may be identified were presented. Once a student is identified for special education, they may have an IEP written and implemented. In this chapter, we discuss and present the various steps and components in IEP implementation and the roles of general and special education teachers in the IEP process.

Steps Prior to IEP Implementation

This section reviews previously presented information necessary to understand how the need for an IEP is established, who is on the IEP team, and whether the IEP is implemented. These steps include (summarized from West Virginia Policy 2419 Regulations for the Education of Exceptional Students (2017), retrieved 05/2020 from https://wvde.us):

1 Parents must be aware of and knowledgeable about their and the school district's rights and responsibilities under IDEA's due process procedures.

2   School districts must give parents prior written notice before all meetings regarding their child's education as it relates to special education.
3   Parents must give consent for an MFE. Parents are also members of the MDET.
4   Individual, nondiscriminatory, reliable, and valid assessments are administered to determine whether a student has a disabling condition, whether the condition adversely affects educational performance, and special education is required.
5   Eligibility is determined by the MDET (or an eligibility committee).
6   Parents must give consent prior to the implementation of an IEP. Parents are members of the IEP team and participate in the development of the IEP. The implementation of the IEP must occur within 90 days of parental consent for the MFE, assuming consent for the IEP.

IEPs are reviewed annually and parents provide consent each year for continued special education services. The MDET conducts a new MFE every three years from the date of the initial identification for eligibility. Whether the IEP is the initial (first) IEP written for a student or is a subsequent annual review, it includes the same elements each year. Some components are required at different ages (e.g., the transition from an Individualized Family Service Plan to an IEP at age three years; transition planning for postsecondary life at age 16 years). Finally, both general and special education teachers will participate in the IEP development initially and each subsequent year (except in the rare instances where there is no *possibility* the student will participate in general education). Due process procedures are followed throughout the student's schooling. The school districts' administrators, teachers, and staff must adhere to the state's policies, procedures and regulations governing all special education processes. In this chapter, forms created by the West Virginia Department of Education (WVDE) will be used as an example IEP. Readers should investigate the IEP forms and regulations in their particular state. These forms and regulations may differ in presentation, but the overall content should be reasonably consistent from one state to the next. Case Study 5.1 will challenge you to review and consider what parents should know prior to their child being evaluated for and provided special education services.

Case Study 5.1

Assume you are a teacher in a school. There is a student you have been working with in class who everyone agrees should be referred for a multi-factor evaluation. You are the student's sponsor teacher and the team asks you to contact the parents before the referral to see what they know about the process and whether they are in agreement. You are not trying to obtain formal consent for the MFE, just helping the parents understand what might happen if they do agree.

1 Go to your state's education department website. Locate the document that is shared with *parents* about special education procedures. It might be entitled something like "Parental rights and responsibilities." Keep in mind this document is likely *not* the same document that education professionals would use to ensure they are following all policies and procedures in the state. The parent document will be in simpler, easier to understand language and will not be as long as the educators' guidelines.

2 What information would you think would be most important to share with parents and/or point out to them to better understand the MFE and IEP processes?

Comprehension Check

1 What steps must occur prior to the implementation of an initial IEP?
2 How often are IEPs reviewed?
3 How often must MFEs be conducted?

Components of the IEP

The completed components of a fictitious IEP will be presented in this chapter. The student, Donald, has an SLD and issues with a language disorder. Summaries of each component are derived from Policy 2419 and West Virginia Special Education Forms and Instructions (2017) (retrieved 05/2020 from https://wvde.us). The figures are derived from the IEP forms used by WVDE.

Important Note to Readers

We acknowledge educators can and do differ in respect to the "correct" way to write an IEP. Be aware that in any particular circumstance, administrators, school districts, and educators may have specific requirements or procedures that can vary from location to location. We also acknowledge our completion and descriptions of each IEP part may differ somewhat from the specific directions of the WVDE. The summaries and descriptions are modified at times to not confuse readers with the tremendous number of details included in each of Policy 2419 and the Special Education Forms and Instructions. Special education teacher candidates, in particular, should be aware that, in any given state, there are detailed directions on how to complete an IEP that go beyond what is included here. These sample IEP parts and descriptions are intended to provide a general knowledge of IEP development and content.

IEP Team Members

The IEP team must include the student's parents, a general education teacher if the student might participate in general education, a special education teacher, a school district representative (usually an administrator), and a professional capable of interpreting evaluation results (e.g., a school psychologist or diagnostician). The IEP team may also include the student, related services personnel (e.g., speech and language pathologist, adaptive physical education teacher), and members of non-school agencies (e.g., early intervention services coordinator, Department of Vocational Rehabilitation caseworker) as consented to by the parents.

IEP teams can be rather large if the student's education and related services are complex, or the team is addressing the transition from early intervention to school-aged services or from secondary to postsecondary living. Of considerable importance is the school district representative (sometimes referred to as the Local Education Agency or LEA representative). Once an LEA representative signs an IEP, the school is then committed to following through on the services outlined in the IEP. While individual team members may dissent with provisions of the IEP, they must abide by what is documented. Parents as individual team members may withhold consent for the implementation of the IEP. In those instances, the IEP is not implemented as written, and the team continues working to develop an agreed-upon IEP.

Parts I and II

Please note that IEPs can be rather complex, and for any given student, the information can differ considerably. However, Figure 5.1 and subsequent Chapter 5 Figures include a "typical" IEP developed for a student participating in the general education classroom and curriculum. An IEP for a student with multiple or severe disabilities may be significantly more involved, and special education teachers will need to know how to facilitate and develop IEPs for students with complex needs and situations. For example, in Part I, a student may have parents who are divorced and living in residences in two different districts, or both parents may have custody and decision-making authority. For the most part, general education teachers will participate in IEP teams for students included for part or most of their school day in the general education settings.

See Figure 5.1 for Parts I and II of a completed IEP, including demographic information.

Figure 5.1 includes essential facts, dates (Part I) and the signature page for attendees (Part II). Of importance in Part I are the annual review date and reevaluation date. The review date is the date of the next IEP annual review and must be within 365 days (one year) of the current IEP review.

INDIVIDUALIZED EDUCATION PROGRAM

Forestville County Schools

Student's Full Name Donald McDonald   **Date** 04/01/2020

PART I STUDENT INFORMATION

Student's Full Name Donald McDonald	Annual Review Date 03/31/2021
School Owl ES	Date of Birth 05/12/2007
Parent(s)/Guardian(s) Peggy and Bill	Grade 5 IEP Grade 5
Address 2333 Woodsy Lane	WVEIS# 1111111
City/State/Zip Forestville, WV 00001	Telephone 304-111-1111

Reevaluation Due Date 09/2022   Exceptionality SLD

Meeting Type: ☐ Initial   ☑ Annual Review

       ☐ Reevaluation   Restart the Annual Review ☐ Yes   ☐ No

       ☐ Other _____   Restart the Annual Review ☐ Yes   ☐ No

Transferred From: _____   Transferred Date: _____

PART II: DOCUMENTATION OF ATTENDANCE

Name	Signature	Position
Peggy Donald		Parent/Guardian
Bill Donald		Parent/Guardian
		Student
Mr. Swanz		General Education Teacher
Ms. Pigeon		Special Education Teacher
Ms Jay, Principal		Chairperson
Mr. Byrd, School Psychologist		
Mr. Robbins Turkey MS Special Education Teacher		
Ms. Eagle Turkey MS General Education 6th Grade Teacher		

The following people participated in the IEP team meeting via an alternate method:

Name	Position	Alternate Method
_____	_____	_____
_____	_____	_____
_____	_____	_____
_____	_____	_____

West Virginia Department of Education
March 2017

Figure 5.1 Parts 1 and II Data and Participants

The reevaluation date is when the subsequent multi-factor evaluation (MFE) (conducted every three years from the initial evaluation) is due. This date may be up to three years in the future. The signature page includes all those who were present or participated by means other than face to face.

Part III Extended School Year Services

Part III is included in Figure 5.2. This part addresses the need for extended school year (ESY) services.

In West Virginia, students who receive IEPs as gifted and talented students (not necessarily students with disabilities), need not be considered for an ESY. It is important to note that not all states develop IEPs for gifted and talented students as they are not covered under the federal IDEA guidelines.

Page ___ of ___

INDIVIDUALIZED EDUCATION PROGRAM

Forestville County Schools

Student's Full Name Donald McDonald   **Date** 04/01/2020

PART III A: EXTENDED SCHOOL YEAR (ESY) DETERMINATION
Will ESY be considered while developing this IEP?
☑ Yes   ☐ No (for gifted only)
The IEP Team in making its determination of a student's need for ESY shall review documentation that the student exhibits, or may exhibit:

- Significant regression during an interruption in educational programming;
- A limited ability to recoup, or relearn skills once programming has resumed;
- Regression/recoupment problem(s) that interfere with the maintenance of identified critical skills as described in the current IEP; and
- Other factors that interfere with the maintenance of identified critical skills as described in the current IEP, such as predictive data; degree of progress; emerging skills and breakthrough opportunities; interfering behaviors; nature and/or severity of the disability; and special circumstances.

(The lack of clear evidence of such factors may not be used to deny a student ESY services, if the IEP Team determines the need for such services and includes ESY in the IEP.)

Does the student need extended school year services?
☐ Yes   ☑ No   ☐ Defer until: _____

PART III B: EXTENDED SCHOOL YEAR SERVICES

ESY Services	Location of Services	Extent/Frequency ____ per ____	Initiation Date m/d/y	Duration m/y

After review of the proposed extended school year services, the parent(s)/guardian(s)/adult student:

☐ accepts extended school services.   ☐ rejects extended school services.

West Virginia Department of Education
March 2017

Figure 5.2 Part III Extended School Year Services

For ESY, the team must consider if summer break away from the school environment is likely to result in significant regression as outlined in the bullet points on the form. If ESY services are warranted, parents may accept or reject the services.

Part IV Consideration of Factors

Figure 5.3 includes an example of Part IV. This part addresses a series of special factors and areas the IEP team should consider before and during the development of the IEP.

Part IV includes a reminder to consider the student's strengths, parental concerns, and special factors in developing the IEP. An IEP is about the *student's best interests* and *parental concerns* about their child's education. These two factors should always be significant considerations in the IEP development. An IEP should not be based solely on *what educators think should happen.* Part IV has a series of factors to be reviewed. If any are checked as "Yes," then those factors must be addressed more fully in the remaining parts of the IEP. Of note is that assistive technology use and support must be considered for every student on an IEP.

Factors do not have to be checked as "Yes" if they can be addressed in the typical instruction routines and the school day. For example, a student may not always complete homework or in-class assignments. The issue is not so severe that the IEP team needs to formally address it since it does not significantly impact the student's own learning or learning of others. The student's teachers may implement an incentive program for all students in the classroom to encourage completion of homework and in-class assignments and monitor all students' progress. In this instance, question 4 (*Does the student's behavior impede his or her learning or that of others?*) can be marked "no" because the behavior is addressed routinely in class. However, question 4 may be marked "yes" if it is clear to the IEP team the student will need special instruction and monitoring.

Part V Assessment Results

Figure 5.4 presents Part V of an IEP which includes assessment results and relevant data used in the IEP development.

The type of assessment data presented on any given student will vary considerably. However, there tend to be specific categories of results consistent across individuals. First are academic achievement test results (also referred to as measures of academic performance/progress – MAPs). Most students on IEPs will take the same bi- or yearly academic achievement tests as their general education peers, although students on IEPs may receive accommodations for these assessments (discussed in Part XI and further in Chapter 6). States administer standardized math and English Language Arts (ELA) assessments in grades 3 through 8. Other

INDIVIDUALIZED EDUCATION PROGRAM

_____ Forestville County Schools

Student's Full Name Donald McDonald   **Date** 04/01/2020

PART IV: CONSIDERATION OF FACTORS FOR IEP DEVELOPMENT/ANNUAL REVIEWS
The IEP team must consider the following factors for all students:
* The strengths of the student.
* The concerns of the parent.
* Results of the initial or most recent evaluation of the student.
If additional evaluations are needed (specify): not at this time
* Academic, developmental and functional needs of the student

Do the following special considerations apply? If yes, document in appropriate section(s) of the IEP.

		YES	NO
1.	Is the student identified as gifted? If yes, consider whether acceleration will be provided and document its effect on graduation.		✓
2.	Does the student need assistive technology devices or services? If yes, document the type of device and provision for home use, if any, and/or the nature and amount of services. Specify: Team has decided audio textbooks for all classes and word processing for writing	✓	
3.	Does the student have communication needs? If yes, address in the IEP.		✓
4.	Does the student's behavior impede his or her learning or that of others? If yes, consider the use of positive behavioral interventions and supports and other strategies to address that behavior.		✓
5.	Does the student have blindness or low vision? If yes, document provision of instruction in braille and the use of braille, or after an evaluation of the student's reading and writing skills, needs and appropriate reading and writing media, including an evaluation of the student's future needs for instruction in braille or the use of braille, document in the present levels a justification that instruction in braille or the use of braille is not appropriate for the student.		✓
6.	Is the student deaf or hard of hearing? If yes, consider the language and communication needs of the student, opportunities for direct communications with peers and professional personnel in the student's language and communication mode, the student's academic level and full range of needs, including opportunities for direct instruction in the student's language and communication mode.		✓
7.	Does the student have limited English proficiency? If yes, consider the student's level of English language proficiency.		✓
8.	Does the IEP team intend to invite a representative from a participating agency to the NEXT IEP meeting to discuss transition services? If yes, written consent must be obtained to invite agency representatives prior to the next IEP meeting and the agency representative must be included on the next IEP meeting notice.		✓
9.	Will this IEP address Transition Services? If yes, the transition planning sections of the IEP must be addressed.		✓

Accessible Educational Materials Guidance
If the student understands instructional content at grade level, but is unable to read with sufficient accuracy and fluency to support comprehension at the same rate as his/her peers; or cannot physically manipulate the print medium; or due to blindness/low vision cannot see standard print materials, please refer to the *Accessible Educational Materials* guidance documents on the WVDE website.

West Virginia Department of Education
March 2017

Figure 5.3 Part IV Factors for Consideration

content areas (e.g., science in Donald's case) are not necessarily assessed statewide on an annual basis. Some schools, districts, or states may also assess early academic skills in grades K-2 or implement content area tests in high school. These assessments help states and districts understand how students are performing in comparison to specific criteria. Individual students and overall class, school, and district performances are tabulated

INDIVIDUALIZED EDUCATION PROGRAM

___Forestville County Schools___

Student's Full Name Donald McDonald   **Date** 04/01/2020

PART V: ASSESSMENT DATA
General Summative Assessment Performance Levels

TEST YEAR	ELA	Math	Science
	Performance Level	Performance Level	Performance Level
2018 3rd grade	Basic	Partial Mastery	
2019 4th grade	Partial Mastery	Mastery	

Alternate Assessment Performance Levels

TEST YEAR	ELA	Math	Science

Interim, Formative, Transition and Additional Assessment Data
Using current, annual data, list the interim, formative and transition assessments that have been used with the student and describe the results and implications for specially designed instruction. This could include data relevant to student behavior, setting demands, work habits/ learning skills, technology skills, workplace skills, independent living skills and performance based assessments. Describe the results and implications for specially designed instruction.

Assessment	Date	Description
WISC V	09/2019	Full scale IQ = 106 (avg)
WJPB	09/2019	Broad reading = SS 80 (below avg), Broad mathematics = 112 (above avg)
		Broad written language = 86 (below avg), Broad knowledge = 104 (avg)
GORT 5	09/2019	GE = 4.1 (below avg)
TOWL 5	09/2019	GE = 3.7 (well below avg)
Current Grades (3rd 9 weeks)	03/27/2020	ELA = C, Science = C, Social Studies = C, Math = B, Art = B, HPE = B

West Virginia Department of Education
March 2017

Figure 5.4 Part V Prior Assessment Results

using various terms such as very good (e.g., advanced, accelerated rank), average (proficient, mastery) or below or well below average (e.g., partial mastery, basic, novice). This data may also be used in part to "grade" schools and districts on their overall academic progress and the performance of minority groups (e.g., African Americans, students with disabilities, low socioeconomic status students). In Figure 5.4, this data for the case study student Donald is presented in the top "box" and identified as General Summative Assessment results. Other states may use a different term for achievement assessments. The student's results for state- and district-wide assessments are typically indicated on their IEP in all states (although in what part or section may differ by state) as an indication of their performance compared to grade-level standards.

In the same figure, the middle "box" includes any data from alternate assessments (discussed in Chapters 1 and 3). When a student has a severe disability, making it unreasonable for them to take the grade-level achievement assessments, even with accommodations, they may be eligible for an alternate assessment. For example, a student with severe disabilities who does not participate in the general education *curriculum* (note: the student may be participating in the general education *classroom* but learning alternate academic standards) may qualify for an alternate assessment as dictated by state policies and procedures. Typically, students taking alternate assessments have more challenging intellectual disabilities or concerns (e.g., severe autism). Depending on the state, a student with disabilities may take both typical (e.g., math) and alternate (e.g., ELA) assessments depending on the content area. Most general education teachers instruct and assist students who take the typical assessments, albeit with accommodations for some. Special education teachers are typically in charge of administering alternate assessments.

Finally, IEP teams may consider other assessment results (included in the lower "box") from multi-factor evaluations, transition planning assessments, speech and language assessments, etc. IEP teams may also wish to include classroom assessments, course or content area grades, and other relevant data. The IEP team needs to understand the student's current academic performance to develop subsequent goals of what the student should know and be able to do before the next annual review.

Part VII will be presented next rather than Part VI. Part VI is focused on transition planning from secondary to postsecondary life. Because this planning is not *required* on an IEP prior to age 16, it will be presented in a latter part of this chapter as this case study student, Donald, is not yet 16 years of age.

Part VII Present Levels of Academic Achievement and Functional Performance

Figure 5.5 presents Part VII: Present Levels of Academic Achievement and Functional Performance. This sample IEP was developed with Donald included in the general education curriculum, and therefore, the present levels reference knowledge and skills related to college and career readiness standards. A later IEP example will present transition planning

_____Forestville County Schools_____

Student's Full Name _Donald McDonald_____   **Date**_04/01/2020_____

PART VII: PRESENT LEVELS OF ACADEMIC ACHIEVEMENT AND FUNCTIONAL PERFORMANCE

Narrative Descriptions of Present Levels of Academic Achievement and Functional Performance (refer to IEP instructions). Include grade level expectations as well as an impact statement which describes how the student's exceptionality will affect access to the general curriculum. Also, include targeted standard(s) where appropriate. Add pages as needed.

Grade Level Expectations:
By the end of 5th grade, students are expected to be able to gather information from content area texts, link that information to prior and future learning, use that information to produce products demonstrating knowledge and skills in their content areas and perform adequately on tests and other measures of academic progress.

Present Level Statement:
Donald demonstrates average intelligence (IQ=106) and broad knowledge (SS = 104). Learning strategy instruction has been identified as helpful in content area learning. He still has difficulty in linking prior and current learning and is disorganized. Donald's reading scores on his MFE indicate his reading and comprehension skills are below average (broad reading SS = 80; Oral reading and comprehension (GE = 4.1). His written language is significantly below grade level (GE 3.7).

Impact Statement:
Learning is more complex and demanding in middle and high school. Donald may fall further behind his peers in acquiring CCRS and his grades may deteriorate despite his gains in 5th grade if he does not continue to learn new strategies for acquiring and using new knowledge and skills and presenting his knowledge and skills in ways that demonstrate he is making adequate progress in the CCRS.

Standards Type: Multidisciplinary evaluation and educational performance data support the following standard type:
- ☑ West Virginia College- and Career-Readiness Standards
- ☐ Alternate Academic Achievement Standards (*This choice MUST be confirmed by checking the box at the bottom of the Alternate Academic Achievement Standards Guidelines page which accompanies Part VII of the IEP*)
- ☐ Early Learning Standards Framework

Targeted Standards:

ELA.5.19
By the end of the year, read and comprehend informational texts, including social studies, science, and technical texts, at the high end of the grades 4–5 text complexity range independently and proficiently.

West Virginia Department of Education
March 2017

Figure 5.5 Part VII Present Levels of Academic Achievement and Functional Performance

for a student who is included in a general education classroom but learning alternate academic standards and functional skills.

Part VII can be conceived as the "justification" for special education services and the need for a particular annual goal. This sample IEP only includes one annual goal. Typically, though, there are several goals on an

IEP, for instance, a separate goal for math, reading fluency, and learning strategies. Each goal area has an individual present level of performance (Part VII) and goal (Part VIII) page. Math has its own Part VII and VIII pages while reading fluency and learning strategies each has its own Part VII and VIII pages.

In Part VII, the first component, *Grade-Level Expectations*, provides the expected performance of a typically developing peer as it relates to the corresponding goal addressed in Part VIII. This section explains what a student who is making adequate progress should know or be able to do at the particular grade level. These expectations are dependent on whether the grade identified in Part I is the present or next grade level. For example, the sample IEPs annual review occurs in April. Since April is toward the end of the school year, much of the instruction will occur in fifth grade rather than the current fourth grade, and therefore, fifth grade standards may be presented.

The second component, *Present Levels Statement*, indicates how the student is performing compared to the grade-level expectations stated above. It should include specific supporting data (e.g., Part VI information, grades, classroom work samples, portfolios, etc.) and *not* merely opinions and observations. It may also include instructional strategies and interventions that have previously been successful. The *Present Level Statement* is a comparison of the student performance to the *Grade Level Expectations*.

The third component, *Impact Statement*, indicates the potential consequence if the student does not have support in reaching the corresponding annual goal. That is, if the student does not make progress over the next year toward meeting grade level expectations, what are the negative implications in terms of the student's progress in the general education curriculum.

The final components, *Targeted Standards*, identifies the corresponding college and career readiness, alternative, or early learning standard the student should be working towards during the IEP's calendar year. At first glance, the need to achieve all grade level standards and expectations may seem obvious, but the IEP teams must prioritize their importance. One area of caution, standards-referenced goals generally should not be so specific that only a single and narrow area of learning is addressed. For example, with Donald, the IEP team identified an ELA standard on reading and comprehending informational texts (identified as *Targeted Standards* in Figure 5.5), which also impacts his performance in math, science, social studies, and so on. Another ELA fifth grade standard is "Analyze how visual and multimedia elements contribute to the meaning, tone, or beauty of a literary text (e.g., graphic novel, multimedia presentation of fiction, folktale, myth, or poem)." While this standard is certainly meaningful, it may be of less concern to Donald's IEP team because of its limited scope and impact on his overall progress in the general education curriculum. Determining these priorities is partly why IEPs are developed by a team rather than one specific individual.

The second standard will still be *taught* to Donald, but the team determined the reading and comprehending information text standard needed addressing through direct and indirect special education and related services.

Readers should also note that goals do not always address areas of "deficiency," particularly as students reach middle or high school grades. Students may have a goal in a content area of strength, especially if it relates to their post-high school transition plans. For example, a student intending to obtain a college degree in creative writing may have a writing goal (an area of strength) related to character and plot development rather than a higher-level mathematics goal. Conversely, a student who wishes to enter the field of engineering would need a higher-level math goal, rather than one related to character and plot development. Both students can benefit from learning in both content areas, but as adulthood nears, the IEP focus further aligns with post-high school transition plans, even if it means some areas receive less attention.

Finally, IEP teams decide whether the student's disability(ies) are such that they will interfere with knowledge and skill acquisition. In these cases, the team may identify appropriate accommodations to compensate for the area of disability rather than focusing instruction in the areas of deficiency. For example, with Donald, the team determined that using audio textbooks as an accommodation would allow him to compensate for reading issues. With the audio textbooks, Donald learns the content without struggling endlessly with the act of reading itself. It doesn't mean the team "gives up" on assisting Donald with improving his reading skills.

Part VIII Annual Goals

Figure 5.6 includes Part VIII of the IEP, the annual goals and objectives.

Annual goals and objectives are instrumental to an IEP. The annual goals identify the focus for special education services (whether delivered in general or special education environments) throughout the duration of the IEP. Short-term objectives (STOs) are the steps or acquired knowledge and skills needed to reach the annual goals. Although only one will be presented here, most IEPs have multiple annual goals. Also, some states or school districts may not *require* STOs if the annual goal directly addresses a college and career readiness standard. STOs are included here as an illustration of how they may be written.

The annual goal and STOs should be "SMART," which is an acronym for:

1   Specific
2   Measurable
3   Ambitious, but
4   Realistic, and
5   Time-oriented.

There are other variations of the SMART acronym, but the essential idea that goals and STOs are specific and measurable is consistent. The IEP in Figure 5.6 is organized as such to promote writing SMART goals as follows:

INDIVIDUALIZED EDUCATION PROGRAM

_____ Forestville County Schools

Student's Full Name Donald McDonald   **Date** 04/01/2020

PART VIII: ANNUAL GOALS with SHORT TERM OBJECTIVES, Part B
(Optional for students who are taught the general standards but is required for students following the WV Alternate Academic Achievement Standards) Add pages as needed.

Critical Skill	Timeframe	Condition	Behavior	Evaluation Procedure with Criteria	Mastery/Progress Codes (optional)
✔	By the next annual review	in social studies and science classes	Donald will independently demonstrate use of learning strategies	as assessed by teacher scored rubrics and class grades.	

SHORT-TERM OBJECTIVES

Critical Skill	Timeframe	Condition	Behavior	Evaluation Procedure with Criteria	Mastery/Progress Codes (optional)
✔	By the end of the 1st 9 weeks of 6th grade	in social studies and science classes	Donald will independently highlight important information in texts	assessed by teacher scored rubrics and class grades.	
✔	By the end of the 2nd 9 weeks of 6th grade	in social studies and science classes	Donald will independently organize present and future learning	assessed by teacher- and self-scored rubrics, and class grades.	
✔	By the end of the 3rd 9 weeks of 6th grade	in social studies and science classes	Donald will independently produce oral and written products	assessed by teacher- and self-scored rubrics, and class grades.	

Progress:

8

How and when will the student's progress toward the IEP goals be reported to the parent(s)? Specify.
How? by written report and report card   When? every 9 weeks

Record dates on which Progress Reports have been provided to parents:

_____   _____   _____   _____   _____   _____   _____   _____

Mastery Code:	0 = Regression	1 = Maintained	2 = Recouped

Student Progress Code:	P = Progress Sufficient	IP = Insufficient Progress A = Achieved	NA = Not Applicable

West Virginia Department of Education
March 2017

Figure 5.6 Part VIII Annual Goals

1   Identify whether the goal is a *critical skill* or crucial to the student's growth and development

2   The *timeframe* is one year or thereabouts for annual goals and potentially shorter periods for STOs

3   The *conditions* are identified under which the performance should be conducted, used, and assessed. In this sample IEP, specific content areas are indicated. Conditions for use and assessment of the goals and STOs are necessary. For instance, demonstrating the use of a learning strategy in a special education environment may be different than doing so in a general education classroom. The demands, distractions, people present, and so on will vary from one classroom or learning situation to the next. Identifying a content area in the sample IEP ensures that the skill will be used and progress monitored in the general education environment.

4   The *behavior* is what the student will be able to do. These (sometimes referred to as target behaviors) should be specific and measurable; for example, a behavior such as "will understand strategies" is neither specific nor measurable. Bloom's Taxonomy, presented in Chapter 8, is often used to identify verbs that emphasize specific and measurable behaviors at various levels of learning.

5   *Evaluation procedures with criteria* indicate how progress will be measured. In this example, one criterion (independently) is included in the behavior. In developing the IEPs, teams are not required to produce the rubrics, datasheets, or other assessment forms that will be used to monitor progress. The team should carefully consider, though, whether the procedures selected align with the target behavior. For example, if the evaluation criteria/procedure for Donald's goal were "with 80% accuracy based on teacher observation," then the evaluation method would be subjective because it does not clearly define the expectations. On the other hand, the use of rubrics as in the sample IEP can be detailed enough to assess the various elements of the behaviors and performance identified in the annual goals and STOs.

6   The *mastery/progress code* indicates the degree of student progress. This part is completed once the IEP is implemented and corresponding instruction provided to indicate the student's level of development or progress. Some states and districts may require the inclusion of actual data in characterizing student progress rather than a code. Other states and districts use alternative forms to document and report a student's progress.

The final aspects of Part VIII include how and when progress will be reported. IDEA requires progress on IEP goals and STOs to be reported at least as often as it is for students without disabilities. IEP teams may elect to report progress as often as report cards are sent to parents or more frequently through means other than report cards (e.g., weekly written reports, monthly parent–teacher conferences).

We acknowledge that some readers may have written these annual goals and STOs differently as to specificity, measurability, and so forth. In these cases, we encourage the readers to rewrite the goals and objectives per their state's or school district's requirements and formatting. Case Study 5.2 will challenge you to write an annual IEP goal.

Case Study 5.2

Assume you are now a teacher for a grade level and content area in which you may be certified/licensed in the future. You have a student in your class who has an IEP. Her annual review will be coming up in about two weeks. The IEP team has asked you to draft an annual goal for the student that is directly related to the content area you are teaching. You know the student is behind her peers and needs to "catch up" by acquiring the most important knowledge and skills for that grade level and content area. The goal should be based on the college and career readiness standards (or similar academic standards) for your state/district.

1   Locate the appropriate standards for the grade level and content area on your state's education department or district website.
2   Write one annual goal for the student that is directly or derived from the academic standards. Why did you pick the standard you did? What makes the standard more important academically in your content area than another standard might be?

Part IX Services

Figure 5.7 includes Part IX of Donald's IEP and includes a description of several different types of services.

Part IX includes three "boxes" that document the services afforded to Donald to help him meet his annual goals. These services are provided along with the assistive technology identified in Part III (*Factors for Consideration*). Recall, factors checked as "yes" in Part III must be addressed in the IEP.

Supplementary Aids, Services/Program Modifications, the first box, are the accommodations, modifications, and additional supports provided to a student with disabilities (accommodations and modifications will be discussed in more detail in Chapter 6). These provisions help a student overcome barriers and remain in the general education environment to the maximum extent appropriate. Donald's IEP team identified word processing technology and audio textbooks in Part III to help him compensate for issues with reading and writing in order to access the general

INDIVIDUALIZED EDUCATION PROGRAM

Forestville County Schools

Student's Full Name Donald McDonald   **Date** 04/01/2020

PART IX: SERVICES

A. Supplementary Aids, Services/Program Modifications	Location of Services	Extent/Frequency	Initiation Date m/d/y	Duration m/y
Audio textbooks	All classes	As needed	04/01/2020	03/2021
Word processing	All classes	As needed	04/01/2020	03/2021

B. Special Education Services	Location of Services	Extent/Frequency	Initiation Date m/d/y	Duration m/y
Learning strategy instruction	Direct GEE	240 minutes/week	04/01/2020	03/2021
	Direct SEE	240 minutes/week	04/01/2020	03/2021
Word processing instruction	Direct GEE	150 minutes/week	04/01/2020	03/2021
	Direct SEE	150 minutes/week	04/01/2020	03/2021

C. Related Services	Location of Services	Extent/Frequency	Initiation Date m/d/y	Duration m/y
AT consultation	Indirect G/SEE	as needed	04/01/2020	03/2020

☐ District and parent agree to waive the 5 day initiation requirement.

West Virginia Department of Education
March 2017

Figure 5.7 Part IX Special Education and Related Services

education curriculum and demonstrate his knowledge and skills in a written format. These are identified again here as supplementary aids available to Donald in all classes on an as-needed basis.

The acronyms GEE and SEE are used to categorize the *Location of Services* as the general education environment (GEE) or special education environment (SEE). Services may be delivered in either or both settings.

The amount of time spent providing services and the initiation and duration dates (not to go past the next annual IEP review date) can vary from service to service.

The second box, *Special Education Services*, documents the special education instruction and services necessary for a student to obtain an appropriate education. In this sample IEP, Part VII and Part VIII (the present levels and annual goals, respectively) identified Donald's need for learning strategies instruction. The IEP team decided Donald would benefit from receiving the instructional services on learning strategies and word processing skills in the resource room (SEE) and support in applying them in general education classrooms (GEE). The SEE would allow for small group instruction on the necessary strategies and skills while in the GEE he can learn to apply them and become a more independent and effective learner.

When the *Location of Services* is "direct," the special education teacher or related service provider is present and working directly with the student. If the service is provided primarily through consultation, it may be considered "indirect." The team believes Donald needs direct SEE services to learn the strategies and skills and apply them in his general education classes.

The third box includes *Related Services*. These are the additional services (e.g., counseling, physical therapy, speech and language pathology services, and special transportation) a student may need to be able to learn and participate in school. Donald's related services include assistive technology (AT), which will be indirectly provided. An AT specialist will consult with his teachers about the appropriate technology and how to teach, apply, and assess its use.

A final box indicates whether the school district and parents waive a 5-day initiation requirement. Waiving this requirement means implementation may occur as soon as possible.

Part IX is *critical*. Whatever is documented as a service in Part IX *must* be delivered. Remember, from Part II, once the district (LEA) representative signs the IEP, they commit the district's resources to fulfilling the specific services identified in the IEP. The IEP does not "guarantee" a student will accomplish the annual goals, but the services and supports identified and documented in the IEP must be delivered.

Part X Least Restrictive Environment

Figure 5.8 includes Part X, placement and the identification of the student's least restrictive environment (LRE). As discussed in Chapter 1, the LRE is the environment where services can be delivered to address annual goals that allow the student to be educated with their nondisabled peers to the maximum extent *appropriate*. Again, the LRE does not require the maximum extent *possible*, but the IEP team must justify why the student needs to be "pulled out" of the GEE for services and consider any potential harmful impact from being pulled out.

Page ___ of ___

INDIVIDUALIZED EDUCATION PROGRAM

_____ Forestville County Schools

Student's Full Name Donald McDonald   **Date** 04/01/2020

PART X: PLACEMENT– Ages 6-21

Explain the extent, if any, to which the student WILL NOT participate in the general education classroom and/or extracurricular and other non-academic activities. Present levels of academic achievement and functional performance must explain why full participation is not possible.

Donald needs individualized instruction in word processing skills and learning strategies in SEE.

Ages 6-21

Total educational minutes per month 7800
Percentage of time in:
80 % General Education Environment   20 % Special Education Environment

		WVEIS LRE Code
☑	General Education: Full-Time (FT) 80% or more	0
☐	General Education: Part-Time (PT) 40% to 79%	1
☐	Special Education: Separate Class (SC) (general education less than 40%)	2
☐	Special Education: Special School (SS) Public or Private	3
☐	Special Education: Out-of-School Environment (OSE)	5
☐	Residential Facility (RF) Public or Private	6
☐	Parentally placed in private school (Service Plan only)	8
☐	Correctional facility	9

Least Restrictive Environment (LRE) Considerations: The IEP team has considered:

☑ Annual placement determination based on IEP.

☑ Only schools and classroom settings appropriate to the student's chronological age.

☑ Education in a general education classroom with the use of supplementary aids and services.

☑ Potentially harmful effects on the selected LRE placement on the student and the quality of the student's services.

☑ Education with age-appropriate non-exceptional peers.

☑ Placement as close to home as possible, in the school the student would normally attend if not exceptional, unless IEP requires other arrangements.

Targeted Case Management may be provided based upon medical necessity
(Not applicable for out-of-state placements)

West Virginia Department of Education
March 2017

Figure 5.8 Part X Least Restrictive Environment

Figure 5.8 includes two major components. The first is the calculation of approximate time spent in the SEE in relation to the total minutes spent in school per month. The total educational minutes per month was determined by multiplying 6.5 hours per school day by 20 school days per month, resulting in 7,800 minutes of school per month.

In Donald's case, the team decided special education services, as documented in Part IX (Figure 5.7), will be equally divided in time between the GEE and SEE. The percentage of time in SEE was then determined by dividing the special education services minutes per week by half (since half are in GEE and half SEE) and then multiplying it by four weeks (the number of weeks per month). With these calculations, Donald would spend about 20% of his time in the SEE. Since he spends 80% of his time in GEE, Donald is considered full time in general education based on the WVDE coding. The code is determined by the percentage of time spent in SEE. Such codes may be used by districts to report to their state the number of students on IEPs, the amount of inclusion provided, and the degree of services needed. In turn, this may affect the funding the state provides to a school district.

The second component is a series of considerations. These are reviewed and checked to ensure the IEP team considers the ramifications of the student's LRE. These considerations are essential to all students but become increasingly important the less time the student spends in the GEE and interacting with peers without disabilities. For example, if the IEP team were to decide a student's LRE was in an alternative school or self-contained SEE, reviewing these considerations would ensure such a decision is in the best interest of the student. An inappropriate LRE decision would be placing a student in an alternative school full-time simply because of a severe disability. Similarly, placing a student in a self-contained SEE classroom full-time would be inappropriate based solely on the teacher's licensure or certification (e.g., prepared to teach the student in particular skills such as American Sign Language or Braille). Again, indirect or direct special education services may be provided and included in the general education environment.

Part XI Statewide Testing Accommodations

Figure 5.9 includes Part XI: Statewide Testing, which addresses the accommodations a student receives when being evaluated through the state- or district-wide assessments. The accommodations identified in this section are typically provided in classes and course-wide assessments as well.

Figure 5.9 includes several important considerations. First is whether the student will take assessments under "standard conditions" (i.e., just the same as all general education students) or "standard conditions with accommodations." This latter designation indicates the student will be assessed on the same knowledge and skills as their grade-level peers but will be provided the accommodations identified in Part XI. Accommodations are categorized as presentation accommodations (how information is presented to the student), response accommodations (how the student will demonstrate knowledge and skills), and timing

INDIVIDUALIZED EDUCATION PROGRAM

_____ Forestville County Schools

Student's Full Name Donald McDonald   **Date** 04/01/2020

PART XI: STATEWIDE TESTING –General Summative Assessment

Indicate the appropriate WV Measures of Academic Progress Assessment (WVMAP) by checking standard conditions or standard conditions w/accommodations.
If the district requires a "District Wide Assessment", all selected WVMAP accommodations apply.

WV-MAP General Assessment: ☐ Standard Conditions   ☑ Standard Conditions w/Accommodations

General Summative Assessment Accommodations (Check all that apply)

PRESENTATION ACCOMMODATIONS:
- ☐ P01 Text-to-speech (excluding ELA passages)
- ☐ P02 Human read aloud (excluding ELA passages)
- ☐ P03 Braille Paper
- ☐ P06 Certified sign language interpreter
- ☑ P13 Documented need text-to-speech (including ELA passages)
- ☑ P14 Documented need human read aloud (including ELA passages)
- ☐ P15 Read aloud directions only
- ☐ P16 Directions presented through certified sign language
- ☐ P17 Braille Online Adaptive (ELA and Math)
- ☐ P18 Simplified Test Directions
- ☐ P19 Paper Version (large print)
- ☐ P21 Screen reading software (JAWS)
- ☐ P22 Enlarge text on screen
- ☐ P23 Magnification device
- ☐ P24 Translator (Human or Electronic) (GSA science only)
- ☐ P25 Electronic translator to present directions (science only)
- ☐ P27 Bilingual word-to-word dictionary
- ☐ P28 High color contrast
- ☐ P29 Sign dictionary to present test, including directions
- ☐ P30 Translated test directions (*Spanish available embedded)
- ☐ P31 Translations glossary (math only)
- ☐ P32 Stacked translations (SPANISH ONLY)
- ☐ P33 Turn off universal tool
- ☐ P34 American Sign Language (ASL)
- ☐ P35 Braille Online Fixed math with tactile graphics provided (ELA - adaptive)
- ☐ P36 Closed captioning
- ☐ P37 Masking
- ☐ P38 Color contrast (color printer required)
- ☐ P39 Color overlays
- ☐ P40 Print on demand (stimuli only)

- ☐ P41 Provide translations glossary (paper-and-pencil tests)
- ☐ P42 Noise Buffers
- ☐ P43 Streamlined Interface
- ☐ P44 Line Reader (ELPA 21 Only)
- ☐ P45 Unlimited replays (ELPA 21 Only)
- ☐ P46 Read aloud in Spanish
- ☐ P47 Alternate Vision Form (DLM Only)

RESPONSE ACCOMMODATIONS:
- ☐ R02 Scribe (excluding ELA full write)
- ☐ R03 Braille response
- ☐ R04 Scribe (including ELA full write)
- ☐ R05 Abacus
- ☑ R11 Assistive technology (Alternate response options)
- ☐ R15 Bilingual word-to-word dictionary
- ☐ R16 Respond in large-print test book
- ☐ R17 Electronic translator to respond
- ☐ R18 Sign dictionary to respond
- ☐ R19 Calculator
- ☐ R20 Multiplication Table
- ☐ R21 Speech-to-text
- ☐ R22 Unlimited re-recordings (ELPA 21 only)
- ☐ R23 100s Number Table

TIMING ACCOMMODATIONS:
- ☐ T03 Take more breaks (no studying) (All WV-MAP tests)
- ☑ T04 Extra time
- ☐ T07 Flexible scheduling
- ☑ T09 Separate setting

West Virginia Department of Education
March 2017

Figure 5.9 Part XI Statewide Testing and Accommodations

accommodations (whether the student needs additional time or setting accommodations). Some states may add setting accommodations separately whereas WVDE has combined timing and setting. Accommodations will be discussed in more detail in Chapter 6. Some accommodations (e.g., Braille) may only be provided to students with particular disabilities.

Text-to-Speech (P13) and Read Aloud (P14) Accommodations for ELA Reading Passages Students with Disabilities Decision Guidance Document

Note: This accommodation is appropriate for a *very small number* of students (estimated to be approximately 1-2% of students with disabilities participating in a general assessment) who have a documented reading disability. Text to-speech is available as an accommodation for students whose need is documented in an IEP or 504 plan.

Student Name: Donald McDonald

Teacher:

YES responses may indicate a need for the text-to-speech (P13) or read aloud (P14) accommodation of ELA Reading Passages. A preponderance of evidence should exist rather than one or two marks in the YES column for the accommodation to be provided.

Questions	Yes	No	Comments
Does the student have a documented reading disability?	✓	☐	
Is the student blind or does the student have a significant visual impairment?	☐	✓	
Is the student a beginning braille reader who has not yet developed braille fluency?	☐	✓	
Does the student have an identified reading-based disability that affects the student's decoding, fluency, or comprehension skills?	✓	☐	Describe skills affected. Difficulty acquiring written information, storing, and retrieval
Have interventions been used to improve the student's decoding, fluency, or comprehension skills?	✓	☐	Describe approaches. Learning strategies instruction
Does the student use text-to-speech or receive a read aloud accommodation during instruction?	✓	☐	word processing software/hardware
Does the student regularly use assistive technology software or audiobooks?	✓	☐	all content area texts are audio
Does the student use text-to-speech or receive a read aloud accommodation during formative assessments or during the WV General Summative Assessment?	✓	☐	
Does someone (teacher, paraprofessional, another student, and parent) regularly read aloud to the student in school?	☐	✓	
Does the student indicate that it is easier to understand a book when it is read aloud by another person or through text-to-speech rather than if they read it independently?	✓	☐	

West Virginia Department of Education
March 2017

Figure 5.9 (continued)

In Figure 5.9, Donald has four accommodations identified. Under presentation accommodations, he will have his tests (including ELA reading passages) text to speech or read aloud. The use of text to speech and read aloud on ELA reading passages (designated as P13 and P14 in Part XI) requires additional documentation found on the second page of Figure 5.9. Please note that ELA assessments can be intended to specifically evaluate *reading* skills, not listening comprehension from a read aloud. Therefore, when the accommodation P13 or P14 is selected, the team must justify why the student should not be required to read the passages independently. Since Donald's IEP team previously identified his struggles with reading and the need for audio textbooks to access information, they were able to justify the P13 and P14 accommodations.

The response accommodation (R11) is identified so that Donald may use word processing to generate any written responses, again, as identified previously on his IEP. The team determined it would be beneficial for Donald to take his assessments in a separate setting (so as not to disturb other students with his presentation accommodations) and with extended time (so he is not "rushed" to complete written assignments in particular).

Part XI is also completed in a similar process for students taking alternate assessments instead of the standardized summative assessments taken by the majority of students.

Part XII Prior Written Notice

Figure 5.10 includes the prior written notice (PWN) provided to parents to summarize the annual IEP review outcomes. Please note a PWN form would be sent before and often after any meeting regarding the student's identification, placement, or education.

PWN is a critical facet of IDEA as parental participation and informed consent are essential principles under that law. PWN must be sent to parents to explain what will happen or did happen at a team meeting (e.g., MDET, IEP team). Note in Figure 5.10, in the paragraph before the LEA representative's signature, the district must ensure parents understand and are informed of their rights and the outcomes of district decisions regarding their child. This assurance may include providing information in the parents' native language and an interpreter if necessary.

Finally, the form may be addressed to the student if they have reached the age of majority. As explained in Chapter 1, a student who has reached the age of majority (typically 18 years) may decide to exercise their rights if the student and parents make this decision.

Finally, parents may be asked to sign a separate consent form, particularly if the IEP meeting is to implement an initial IEP. This consent form indicates parents agree to and accept the provisions outlined in the IEP including any SEE placement. In following annual reviews, agreeing with continuing the updated IEP continues parental consent. However, parents could withdraw consent at an annual review if they disagree with or are no longer interested in their child receiving special education and related services.

An additional IEP form will be presented addressing transition planning. This form will reference a fictitious student named Peter rather than Donald, as Donald has not reached the age when transition planning must begin (age 16 years).

Page ___ of ___

INDIVIDUALIZED EDUCATION PROGRAM

_____ Forestville County Schools

Student's Full Name Donald McDonald   **Date** 04/01/2020 _____

PART XII: PRIOR WRITTEN NOTICE OF DISTRICT'S PROPOSAL/REFUSAL

Dear Parent/Adult Student:

As a result of:
- ☐ a Student Assistance Team (SAT) meeting conducted on _____,
- ☐ an Eligibility Committee (EC) meeting conducted on _____,
- ☑ an Individualized Education Program (IEP) Team meeting conducted on 04/01/2020 _____,
- ☐ a disciplinary action occurring on _____,
- ☐ other _____,

The district is ☑ proposing or ☐ refusing to initiate or change:
- ☐ the educational evaluation or reevaluation of the student.
- ☐ the identification of the student as having a disability.
- ☐ the educational placement of the student.
- ☑ the provision of a free appropriate public education (FAPE) to the student.

Specifically, the district is:

Implementing push-in and pull-out services in sciences and social studies and other content area courses as needed for learning strategies instruction, AT consultation, word processing
The district is ☑ proposing or ☐ refusing this action because:
These services will allow Donald to access and perform in the general education curriculum.

The evaluation procedure(s), assessment(s), record(s) or report(s) the district used as a basis for the
☑ proposed or ☐ refused action include:
MFE results, report card, classroom assessment results, GSA results
Other options the district considered, but rejected include:
The reasons the above options were rejected include:
Other factors relevant to the district's ☐ proposal or ☐ refusal include:

Exceptional students and their parents have protections under the procedural safeguards. A copy of the Procedural Safeguards Brochure and assistance in understanding the provisions of the procedural safeguards may be obtained by contacting the Director of Special Education at Forestville _____, if available, the local Parent Educator Resource Center at Forestville _____ and/or the West Virginia Department of Education, Office of Special Education at 304.558.2696 or 1.800.642.8541.

Sincerely,

LEA representative   04/01/2020
Signature/Position   **Date**

West Virginia Department of Education
March 2017

Figure 5.10 Part XII Prior Written Notice

Transition Planning Forms

Figure 5.11 is a sample Part VI: Transition Planning, completed on Peter, a student with more severe disabilities. Transition planning is required for *all* students with an IEP no later than age 16 years.

INDIVIDUALIZED EDUCATION PROGRAM

Forestville   County Schools

Student's Full Name Peter Peterson   **Date** 04/2020

PART VI: TRANSITION PLANNING
(For students beginning no later than the first IEP to be in effect when the student is 16, or younger if appropriate)
(Refer to Policy 2419, 2510, and IEP instructions)

Age of Majority
The student and parent have been informed of the transfer of educational rights that will occur on reaching age 18

☑ Yes ☐ No   Date 02/24/2020

Student Initials PP   Parent/Guardian Initials FP & MP
NOTE: *Age of Majority brochure is available on the WVDE website.*

Transition Planning Considerations:
How were the student's preferences and interests considered?
☑ Student interview/survey   ☐ Interest inventory   ☑ Parent interview/survey   ☑ Functional vocational evaluation

Transition Assessments Reviewed (specify):
Performance-based community-based assessments in addition to above

The student's educational program will lead to a: ☐ standard diploma ☑ alternate (modified) diploma
NOTE: *Alternate (Modified) Diploma brochure is available on the WVDE website.*

Appropriate measureable postsecondary goals based upon age appropriate transition assessments:
1. Education/Training Goals:
   Peter will engage in community-based vocational training.
   Peter will apply to be a voc rehab client.
2. Employment Goals:
   Peter will obtain a social security card.
   Peter will obtain a monthly bus pass.
3. Independent living skills goal(s) (if appropriate):
   Possible assisted living arrangements be investigated.

Select one of the following Career Clusters:

☐ Agriculture, Food and Natural Resources
☐ Business Management and Administration
☐ Government and Public Administration
☐ Human Services
☐ Manufacturing
☐ Transportation, Distribution and Logistics

☐ Architecture and Construction
☐ Education and Training
☐ Health Sciences
☐ Information Technology
☐ Marketing
☐ Arts, A/V Technology and Communication

☐ Finance
☐ Hospitality and Tourism
☐ Law, Public Safety, Correction and Security
☐ Science, Technology, Engineering and Mathematics
☐ Cluster Undetermined (*Option for Grade 7 or below*)

Specify the program of study that aligns with the career cluster the student selected: _____

West Virginia Department of Education
March 2017

1

Figure 5.11 Part VI Transition Planning

INDIVIDUALIZED EDUCATION PROGRAM

<u>Forestville</u>   County Schools

Student's Full Name <u>Peter Peterson</u>   **Date** <u>04/2020</u>

Select one of the following program of studies which aligns with the student's chosen career cluster and provides the best option for success in the global workplace and postsecondary education.

☐ **State-Approved Career and Technical Education (CTE) Program of Study** is an approved sequence of four CTE courses which align to a CTE cluster and pathway, impacts state economic labor market needs as verified by Workforce data and leads to an industry-recognized credential or certificate or opportunity for continuing into postsecondary level education. Students must be capable of passing 100% of the safety exams for the respective program of study.

☐ **State-Approved Individual Work Readiness Competencies (IWRC)** - *Preequisites: Before selecting IWRC, students must have initially selected the State-Approved (CTE) Program of Study option; completed at least two CTE courses in their chosen area of career interest; passed ALL safety exams; demonstrated the ability to acquire basic/core CTE skills at an entry level; were unable to master ALL of the required skill sets associated with their state-approved CTE program of study.*

IWRC is an approved sequence of four CTE courses which align to a CTE cluster and pathway that provides students with a current IEP the opportunity to gain valuable work readiness through a CTE program of study. Students demonstrate the necessary skill sets for entry level support jobs in a specific occupational area. Students must be pursuing a standard diploma and be capable of passing 100% of the safety exams for the respective program of study.

☐ **State-Approved Career Integrated Experiential Learning (CIEL)** a CTE program of study that provides opportunities for students to test for multiple nationally recognized certifications while earning credit for relevant job-readiness skills. CIEL can only be initiated at the Office of Diversion and Transition. CIEL credits will transfer to the receiving high school allowing for the continued enrollment for graduation credit.

☐ **Locally Developed Career and Technical Education (CTE) Program of Study** is a locally approved sequence of four CTE courses which align to a CTE cluster and pathway, impacts a local economic labor market need as verified by local advisory council and leads to an industry-recognized credential or certificate or opportunity for continuing into postsecondary level education.

☐ **Locally Developed Personalized Program of Study** is a locally approved sequence of four courses which align to a career cluster and a program of study that could lead directly to an industry-recognized certificate or license or credit-bearing academic college courses. Best practice would be to encourage college bound students to take at least 1 (one) AP and/or AC course with corresponding examination, a fourth science or computer science credit, and 2 credits in one world language.

☑ **Locally Developed Community Ready Program of Study** is a locally approved sequence of four courses which align to a career cluster that will lead to placement in entry-level support jobs or workforce training programs.
☐ **Undetermined** – Option for Grade 7 or below

Specific course selections must be documented in the student's Personalized Education Plan (PEP) in collaboration with the school counselor, teachers, advisors and parent/guardian. A copy of the PEP must be kept with student's IEP.

West Virginia Department of Education
March 2017

Figure 5.11 (continued)

Activities/Linkages: Identify activities needed for attaining postsecondary outcomes and the lead party/agency responsible for those services.

Activities/Linkages	Parent/ Student	School	Agency (Specify)	Description of Service	Annual Goal to Support Activity
	Lead Party/Agency				
Instruction/education	☐	☑	☐	CBI in work sites	☐
Vocational aptitude/interest assessment	☐	☐	☐		☐
Career awareness/work-based learning	☐	☑	☑	school & DVR - voc rehab client	☐
Employment	☐	☑	☑	career development/	☐
Independent living/mobility	☑	☐	☐	bus pass, social security, assisted living	☐
Agency referral/application	☑	☐	☑	Social security	☐

West Virginia Department of Education
March 2017

Figure 5.11 (continued)

Peter is a student with a severe intellectual disability. He has been learning alternate academic standards throughout his schooling, including inclusive community-based instruction to acquire functional living and work skills. As he has progressed to middle and high school, he has spent less time in GEEs and more time in community-based instruction.

In transition planning, IDEA requires the IEP team to address three areas:

1   Postsecondary education/training
2   Employment
3   Independent living (as appropriate).

Since Peter has a severe disability, it is appropriate for the team to address his independent living concerns. A student with milder disabilities (such as Donald when he becomes 16 years of age) may be determined capable of living independently similarly to students without disabilities.

On this plan, the team identifies considerations, reviews assessments, and documents the type of diploma the student will earn (note: not all states may offer alternative diplomas for students with severe disabilities). The considerations include various types of transition assessments that will be used to determine the student's interests, aptitudes, and both student and parent preferences.

Districts often have vocational programs to prepare students, including those with disabilities, for a career or field that may lead to specific national or state certifications and programs of studies identified by departments of education. There is a wide variety of areas of such programs. These programs may be delivered through Career Technical Education (CTE) in the local high school or a CTE school operated by several districts in collaboration. Such schools are sometimes referred to as career, technical, or vocational schools. These schools typically provide the students' education in the final two years of high school and include academic, career, and technical courses. Students with more severe disabilities may be included in such programs (e.g., hospitality, early childhood education), or they may have an individually determined program as with Peter.

Locally developed programs allow districts to prepare students for adult working and living in the local economy and community. They do not generally lead to national or state certifications (e.g., in airplane maintenance, engineering). For example, the district serving Peter may identify a particular industry (e.g., tourism or hospitality) that is a major aspect of the local economy. Although Peter may not have the ability to complete a certification program in that area, he may have on-the-job training and support while in high school to prepare him for a specific job(s) in that area. For example, Peter's special education teacher and support personnel (e.g., adult service agencies) may educate and train Peter to work in a restaurant. He may greet and seat customers, prepare salads, set tables, set up beverages, and wash dishes. Similarly, Peter might be educated in providing services to mechanics such as locating tools, bringing supplies, assisting with repairs, assisting customers, etc. in a local automobile tire and repair shop. If Peter could alphabetize and perform other clerical duties, he might work in a local business filing, printing, mailing, greeting clients, and so on. Peter might also be involved in learning duties at a local hospital. Deciding the student's education for postsecondary life and employment should be based on student and parent interests and preferences. It should not *just* be based on what professionals think is appropriate (e.g., only food service or custodial work).

Some community colleges and universities provide postsecondary programming for students with disabilities to learn life, social, and career skills. These programs may be residential as with students without disabilities. Also, students may enroll in postsecondary education, such as apprenticeship programs for career education. What is most important is that students be given options and opportunities to continue to develop after high school and not "fall through the cracks," leaving parents alone to navigate through the world of adult services providers and programs.

Activities that address the three areas identified should be specified, along with who will be responsible for conducting those activities. For Peter, there are activities in each of the three areas and the person responsible, including school and agency personnel (e.g., Division of Vocational Rehabilitation – DVR), as well as Peter and his family. Transition planning is critical to successful (and less social services dependence) adult outcomes. The transition plan identifies the appropriate measurable postsecondary goals for the student in Part VI prior to the present levels and annual goals (Parts VII and VIII) sections. This is because planning for adult life from age 16 years on should be of high priority.

For Peter, the team might identify functional annual goals such as:

1 By the next annual review, at work, Peter will converse with others (customers, co-workers) independently as evaluated by observation and checklists of conversational skills.
2 By the next annual review, while going to and from work, Peter will ride a city bus independently as evaluated by a task-analysis and levels of prompting data.

Peter (and other students with mild to more severe disabilities) might also have behavioral goals.

1 By the next annual review, when given feedback by a teacher or supervisor, Peter will react by yelling, stomping his feet, and walking away no more than once per month as evaluated by observation and anecdotal recordings of the situation (where, when, in what circumstances), who offered the criticism, how Peter responded, and how the teacher/supervisor responded.

Having the transition plan and annual goals encourages the team to truly consider Peter's and his parents' wishes for an education that will promote successful adult outcomes. These goals are not required to be strictly academic and may incorporate knowledge and skills regarding behavior, social skills, communication, functional academics, community life, employment, and other areas of functional skills. Students such as Donald, as needed, may also have annual goals addressing areas outside of actual academic knowledge and skills.

Comprehension Check

1 Who are the required members of an IEP team?
2 How are present levels of achievement and performance related to the annual goals?
3 How are annual goals related to the services identified in Part IX?

Roles of General and Special Education Teachers

Special education teachers are often the "case manager" for a group of assigned students with IEPs. Depending on the district size and resources, the special education teacher may be responsible for:

1 Completing all PWN to parents and ensuring all timelines for completion of IEPs are met
2 Conducting assessments for an MDET and collecting data on present levels of student achievement and performance
3 Contacting parents and students to obtain input regarding preferences, interests, concerns, etc., before the meeting
4 Collecting data and informing general education teachers and related services personnel about policies and procedures
5 Leading the IEP meeting and being the primary recorder and "writer" of the final IEP
6 Ensuring regular assessments are conducted to measure progress and progress reports are provided as prescribed in the IEP to parents
7 Ensuring parents and students know and understand their rights and responsibilities under IDEA and will or did occur in a meeting
8 Providing direct and indirect services in special and general education classrooms
9 Collaborating with general education teachers to plan, deliver, and assess students in the general education curriculum.

This list is not exhaustive. The larger a school district and the more personnel involved (particularly if there is a special education director and supporting staff), the more responsibilities are delegated among various educators. However, special education teachers are members of IEP teams. They will consult with parents, students, and general education teachers, collect relevant data, develop preliminary goals and objectives prior to the meeting, conduct and lead the meeting or at least the discussions regarding goals and services, provide direct and indirect services, and collaborate with general education teachers, related services personnel, administrators, parents, and possibly non-school agency personnel.

General education teachers may be less involved than their special education colleagues in the mechanics, due process procedures, and documentation included in the IEP. General education teachers will:

1 Collaborate with special education and related services colleagues, students, parents, and administrators to plan, deliver, and assess instruction
2 Collect data related to progress in the general education curriculum and present achievement and performance levels, including possibly IEP goal progress data
3 Devise teaching and intervention strategies to overcome student challenges
4 Provide accommodations during instruction and possibly assessments as well
5 Promote the social and academic inclusion of students with IEPs
6 Participate meaningfully in team meetings regarding the education of students with IEPs.

Both special and general education teachers should assume advocacy roles to promote their students' best interests in school and adult life after school. Collaboration is mandatory for the successful education and inclusion of students with disabilities in schools and communities.

Comprehension Check

1 What are three important responsibilities special education teachers may assume in the development and implementation of IEPs?
2 What are three important responsibilities general education teachers may assume in the development and implementation of IEPs?
3 Why should both general and special education teachers assume the role of an advocate?

References

West Virginia Board of Education (2017). Special Education Process Forms with Instructions. Retrieved from www.wvde.us, 05/2020.
West Virginia Board of Education (2017). Policy 2514 Regulations for Education of Exceptional Students (with revisions). Retrieved from www.wvde.us, 05/2020.

6 Teaching Strategies

Catherine Lawless Frank

Objectives: After reading this chapter, students will be able to:

1 Identify placement options
2 Understand teaching strategies that support all learners including those with disabilities and other diverse learning needs
3 Discuss the differences between accommodations and modifications
4 Explain the purpose of a 504 Plan.

The previous chapters discussed laws, support systems, disability characteristics, determining eligibility, and IEPs. This chapter will examine teaching strategies and frameworks for accommodations and modifications designed to support students with disabilities and other diverse learning needs. In any classroom, there is a multitude of different learning styles, strengths, and needs. The pedagogies discussed in this chapter address this diversity in general education classrooms and are not just for students with disabilities. Students learn in different ways and achieve at different paces, but all students progress given the right supports.

Placement of Students

By law, students with disabilities are educated in their least restrictive environment (LRE) alongside their general education peers to the maximum extent appropriate. Chapter 1 discussed the continuum of services and presented the array of possible placements for students with disabilities. In most K-12 schools, the LRE can be conceived through three broad approaches:

1 full inclusion in the general education classroom
2 resource room placement that is part-time special education along with general education placement
3 self-contained classroom placement that is predominately special education placement with opportunities to socialize with nondisabled peers during specials, lunch, and other non-academic activities.

The IEP team is responsible for determining which is the appropriate LRE for the individual student. As discussed in Chapters 1 and 5, the LRE is determined by whether a student is attending the school they would attend if they had no disability, whether they are being educated with nondisabled, chronological age peers, whether special education services can be delivered in the general education classroom, and whether any "pull out" services are clearly in the student's best interests.

Full Inclusion

In full inclusion, all instruction, including general and special education and related services, is provided in the same classroom. Students with disabilities are educated alongside their general education peers all day, and special education services are "pushed in" or provided within that environment. A special education teacher may co-teach for part or all of the school day (see Chapter 7). Related services personnel (e.g., a speech and language pathologist or occupational therapist) may provide individualized student support. A paraprofessional may assist an individual or group and work alongside the general education teacher. In full inclusion, students with disabilities remain with their general education peers throughout the school day, and the needed specially designed instruction is provided within that environment.

Resource Room

A second manner of providing special education services is the resource room or pull out approach. Here the student spends most of their time alongside their general education peers but receives some or all of their special education services in a resource room or other pull out environment such as a sensory room. The resource room approach provides individualized or small group instruction on academic areas (typically language arts or mathematics), a related service (such as speech and language or physical therapy), or behavior management (social skills class or anger management). These short pull out sessions (generally no more than 1 hour) provide specialized instruction. The student then spends the remainder of the day receiving the majority of the instruction, usually based on the college and career readiness standards, alongside their general education peers.

Self-contained Classroom

The final approach is a self-contained classroom. Here the student receives all or most of their instruction in a special education environment. This approach is the most restrictive and reserved for the small number of students with the most significant needs. Students spend all or most of their day with other students with special needs in classes designed to meet their more intensive academic, adaptive living, medical, and behavioral concerns. However, students in self-contained classrooms may be integrated with general education peers during non-academic activities such as lunch, perhaps music or art classes, whole school activities such as field days, and extra-curricular activities.

The vast majority of students with special needs spend part or all of the school day in the general education environment. Classrooms have diverse learners even if there are no students on IEPs. Every student has different background knowledge, experiences, learning styles, strengths, and needs. The wide range of abilities, skills, and interests in a classroom makes it imperative for teachers to develop strategies to engage and support learners. Teachers must be able to adapt to the varying demands of their students and ensure all students are engaged and learning. The teaching strategies identified below support differences in learners and not just those with disabilities.

Comprehension Check

1   Who determines a student's LRE?
2   What is full inclusion? What are "push in" services?
3   How do resource room and self-contained placements differ?

Teaching Pedagogies

Direct instruction is a commonly used (and often misunderstood teaching framework) designed to systematically lead students toward a level of mastery and reinforces necessary skills and concepts with different pacing as needed. Sheltered instruction, designed for English Learners, clarifies language and content for all students focusing on acquisition and application of academic language, concept, and skill development. Universal Design for Learning is used for providing multiple means of engagement, representation, and action and expression. None of these frameworks is specifically designed for students with disabilities and can provide equal access to content and instruction, individualization, and opportunities for all students to demonstrate what they have learned.

Direct Instruction

Direct instruction involves explicitly teaching a set of skills through a structured step by step process (Gersten, Woodward, & Darch, 1986). This approach supports diverse student needs and is useful for teaching a wide variety of skills, such as reading comprehension, writing concepts, and mathematical processes. Lessons are structured to enhance content, scaffold skill development, and provide supportive instruction and student feedback. It explicitly communicates what the students should know and be able to do to independently and accurately acquire knowledge and skills. There are a variety of direct instruction models (such as "I do, We do, You do"), but the basic structures and concepts are the same. The four-phase example below demonstrates the foundations of this approach.

1   *Orientation/Anticipatory Set.* In the beginning, a rationale and purpose are provided to "hook" or engage students and make the content important and relevant to students. Background knowledge is primed, and connections made to previous learning and future content ("Last week we learned about ...," "This relates to what we will be studying next week, which is ..."). Orienting the students to the lesson fosters motivation and connects new learning to relevant prior knowledge. This phase is particularly helpful when the teacher can illustrate or engage students in why the learning is important and how it will impact them in positive ways. For example, "Today we are going to begin learning to write paragraphs. Where have we read a paragraph recently? When do you think you will ever need to write a paragraph? What does a paragraph look like when you read it? How is it different than a sentence?" and so on.

2   *Presentation.* The objective and content are then explicitly taught and how, when, and why to use the information is demonstrated and modeled. Using multiple means of instructions (visual, auditory, hands-on, thinking aloud), providing structural supports (guided notes, highlighting key concepts), and formatively assessing student learning throughout increases comprehension of the material. Often referred to as the "I do" phase, the information is explicitly taught and modeled by the teacher. In expanding the paragraph example from above, the teacher may provide the following presentation.

> "Well, a paragraph is more than one sentence, it is indented at the beginning, and all the sentences are tied to one topic. I will show you some examples. Who can point to the indenting? How many sentences are in the paragraph? Read it and see if you can tell me what the topic is (what it is about)?"
>
> "Now, I am going to write a paragraph. I need to pick a topic first ... I need to indent. Now I will write my first sentence. I have to keep it on topic."

In this phase, the emphasis is on students being able to recognize the relevant aspects of the learning and then be able to verbally explain how those aspects work. Being able to "tell themselves about writing a paragraph" is more important at this point than actually writing the paragraph. The teacher wants the students to develop an internal voice regarding steps in the learning without being burdened with actually performing the task. Students are asked throughout the phase to "Show me .... Find the .... Point to .... Tell me ...." Teachers may state "I want each of you to turn to your partner and tell them all the steps in writing a paragraph. Neighbors, check to see if they tell you all the steps. Then, you tell your neighbor the steps and they can check you."

3   *Structured Practice.* Once taught, students complete the task with direct supervision, guidance, and feedback to ensure a clear understanding. This guided practice is the "We do" step in which the teacher and students perform the task together, allowing for scaffolding of knowledge and immediate teacher feedback.

> For example, "Now you are going to write a paragraph. What do you need to do first? Okay, now that you have a topic, write the first topic sentence. Remember, what do you do with the first sentence – that's right – indent. I'll give you two minutes to write your topic sentence. Read your topic sentence to your neighbor and see if they understand your topic. Who has questions? Let me hear some of you read your sentences. Others come to the board and write your topic sentence."
>
> The teacher continues to lead the students through each step of the task, repeatedly asking them to explain what they are doing and why. The teacher praises correct responses and offers corrective (but not negative) feedback. Students can act as peer helpers as they move forward. The teacher in this example would have students take multiple opportunities to write paragraphs under the teacher's observation and direction and allow students to work with peers to achieve understanding.

4   *Independent Practice.* Once a substantial number of students in the class can successfully complete the task together, students independently practice and reinforce the skill. That is, students should not be asked to move ahead to do the task by themselves until the teacher is confident they can complete it with no or only very minor errors. Independent practice, or "you do," should only be provided after the students have demonstrated a degree of mastery and received specific feedback as to what the students are doing correctly and incorrectly. If the teacher moves students to independent practice too quickly, the students may actually practice various "errors" in the task. This can lead to confusion about the correct order of or procedures in the task, making it more difficult for the task to be learned correctly. The early acquisition of the internal voice should help students mentally "walk themselves through" the skill. The independent practice results guide future instruction and determine whether the content has been mastered or needs to be revisited or

retaught. The teacher may also identify those students in need of additional instruction and provide small group or individual support.

For example, "Steve, Katie, and Geoff, I would like for you to come over to this table to be with me. Others, I want you to write a paragraph by yourself. If you get stuck, you can still ask a peer for help but try to do it by yourself first. We'll check everyone's work after 8 minutes." The teacher then takes her small group (where she can still visually monitor the other students), and works with them to provide further instruction in the area of need with corrective feedback. The teacher may say,

"You are writing more than one sentence, but your sentences are not always on the same topic. So, let's work on writing one topic sentence. Tell me your topic and then begin. Remember to do what? Indent, that's right! Now that you have finished your topic sentence, let's read those to ourselves and see if they make sense and then let's read one another's."

The teacher also occasionally checks to see if those working independently are on-task and/or have completed their work.

"Oh Connie, I see you have finished. Ask Treavor to read yours and you read Treavor's to see if the paragraph makes sense. Tell each other what you think is right or if anything needs more work." "As we wrap up this lesson, I want someone to tell me what you learned today. Why is it important? What are the steps you followed? Turn in your work and tomorrow, we will continue to work on writing paragraphs!"

The identification of which students are in which phase of instruction and learning guides the teacher in devising groups, setting up peer modeling and tutoring, or bringing in a co-teacher or aide to assist with groups.

Students who have clearly mastered the new skill can independently practice previously mastered skills or learning can be accelerated for them. For instances, the teacher from the previous examples may say: "You four have really done a great job of writing a paragraph. Tomorrow, I think you can work in pairs to see if you can write a paragraph of at least five sentences and two or even three paragraphs on the same topic!" Or, the teacher could enrich learning for advanced students and tell them, "I want you to use your laptops to look up information about …. Then, you are going to write a paragraph or two in pairs about what you found out" (e.g., Where do birds go in winter? What is important about the state capitol? Who was Dr. Seuss?).

The direct instruction method is sometimes misrepresented as completely teacher-led instruction such as a lecture followed by a quiz. This is simply incorrect. In each phase, the teacher uses peer supports, models, and tutoring as appropriate to help students learn from each other. In fact, direct instruction relies on students helping one another. A fellow student may be better able to demonstrate, model, or explain a task in a way that is understandable to another student than the teacher.

Direct instruction provides a framework for explicit teaching so students can master skills and retain information. It is designed to scaffold instruction, allow for individualized pacing and skill acquisition, and encourage collaborative work. The process provides specific feedback on what is being done correctly and helps when something is amiss. Direct instruction works to ensure all students, including those with disabilities, acquire the "must-have" skills (e.g. addition, subtraction, writing, alphabetic principles, beginning reading skills). These must-have skills may very well be the ones struggling students need to make adequate progress.

Direct instruction is not always the best teaching approach for every lesson, but it provides focused instruction on the essential skills that all learners must learn and do. Direct instruction can complement other teaching approaches, and educators should never "marry" themselves to one method. It supplements methodologies such as discovery learning, problem-solving approach, and project-based learning. The two other approaches discussed here, sheltered instruction and Universal Design for Learning, are also useful for classrooms with diverse student populations.

Sheltered Instruction

An instructional framework designed for English Learners (EL), including those with disabilities and other diverse learning needs, is sheltered instruction. Sheltered instruction, through programs like Sheltered Instruction Observational Protocol (SIOP), builds on direct instruction to assist students in language development while learning academic content. Objectives for both content and language development are incorporated into lessons to stretch students' abilities and foster increased language acquisition (Iris Center, 2011).

For example, in a science lesson on classifying rocks, objectives would include the types of rocks (igneous, metamorphic, and sedimentary) and the language demands necessary to successfully differentiate and identify the rocks (volcano, sediment, layers, heat, pressure). The language objective and supports are differentiated based on individual student needs. Contextual supports (pictures, tables, graphs, guided notes), activating background knowledge (questioning, brainstorming, making explicit connections), and teaching academic language and vocabulary assist in bridging language barriers. This approach requires teachers to have a firm grasp of students' linguistic abilities to provide the appropriate supports that facilitate language acquisition and the development of content knowledge.

It is important to note that language barriers exist for a variety of reasons and not just EL. Recall from Chapter 4 that many students with disabilities have a secondary language disorder. A language disorder involves processing spoken and/or written language (reading) and expressing oneself orally or in writing. Therefore, the sheltered instruction approach can address issues concerning language disorders. It supports the diversity in student backgrounds, which also impacts language acquisition, including those without disabilities and for whom English is their native language. Focusing on academic language and other linguistic demands helps bridge these differences for all students. In the science lesson, all students have to integrate new meanings of layers, heat, pressure, and rocks into their existing concepts and understand that language can have different meanings based on the context.

Universal Design for Learning

Universal Design for Learning (UDL) is a brain-based research pedagogy that incorporates supports and strategies so all students have equal access to learning. It builds upon direct and sheltered instructions to help students overcome barriers through enhancing engagement, diversifying teaching strategies, and facilitating the demonstration of student knowledge. UDL allows teaching, learning, and engagement to happen in multiple ways within the same lesson. For example, Aurora struggles to read. In history class (and all classes), she has difficulty successfully comprehending and completing history lessons that require reading. Aurora's failure to learn history is primarily due to reading difficulties, which cause her to be unable to access (or read) the information or textbook. Her challenges in history relate directly to her struggles with reading. Reading interferes with her learning the content and completing assignments. When there are options or multiple means of representation of the history material (audio textbooks, text to speech, guided notes, and videos), Aurora, and all students, can access the content and learn history through their preferred means without interference or barriers. Through UDL practices, the ability to learn history is not dependent on the ability to read. Aurora and her classmates are also more likely to be engaged (and better behaved) in a classroom where they have the means to access and learn the material in a manner that supports their skills, needs, and interests. Teachers are often unaware of the barriers students face, such as difficulties with memorization, socio-emotional concerns, and lack of background or vocabulary knowledge. UDL calls for intentionally implementing supports to help all students overcome these barriers and become active learners.

There are three main principles of UDL which allow students to engage, access, and demonstrate knowledge by providing variation in teaching practices and supports. The three principles are multiple means of engagement, multiple means of representation, and multiple means of action and expression. These principles consist of 31 individual "checkpoints" that provide specific ideas and strategies for teachers. These principles and checkpoints can be integrated throughout a lesson to promote engagement, access to learning, and facilitate the demonstration of student knowledge (CAST, 2018).

Multiple means of engagement is the "why" of learning and is used to increase motivation and stimulate student interest. This principle aims to develop learners who are purposeful and motivated by fostering student interests in learning, nurturing persistence and effort, and advancing self-regulation of thoughts, behaviors, and emotions. Engagement is cultivated by incorporating student choices, varying instructional demands, and enhancing the content's relevance. Emphasis is placed on building a classroom community, providing supports for students' self-regulation, and providing specific frequent feedback on both academic and behavioral strengths and areas of need (CAST, 2018).

Multiple means of representation are the "what" of learning and incorporate the lesson's objective and procedures. Since students' learning styles and strategies differ, this principle offers variation in how materials and content are presented and enhanced to be accessible for all students. The goal is to develop resourceful and knowledgeable students by incorporating alternative ways of receiving or inputting and perceiving the content. It includes support for understanding language, features, and symbols, and reinforcing comprehension. Multiple means of representation include visual supports, closed captioning, transcripts for videos and auditory materials, explaining and highlighting vocabulary, formulas, patterns, syntax and structure, and activating background knowledge. Structuring supports and clarifying content makes learning accessible and increases comprehension (CAST, 2018).

Multiple means of action and expression are the "how" of learning and how students demonstrate what they know. Rather than relying on pen and paper, UDL advocates for differing modes of assessment that produce strategic and goal-directed learners. Students demonstrate their knowledge through the uses of physical actions and increased options for expression and communication with an emphasis on executive functioning skills. It advocates for variety and choice in assessments that demonstrate knowledge, enhance thinking skills, and circumvent barriers that result from deficiencies in skills and a lack of student interest (CAST, 2018).

Case Study 6.1 UDL Illustration

When Tameka prepares for her literacy class, she aligns the content with the college career and readiness standards and her students' needs. Tameka begins each lesson by developing the students' background knowledge on the topic, determining what they know and how the content is relevant to their lives and future learning.

She stated the objective for the class and posted it and the class schedule on the board.

Depending on the objective for the day, Tameka provides choices and integrates supports. When she assigns readings in class or for homework, she provides access to text to speech computer software and provides clarifying questions, graphic organizers, or guided notes. She integrates reviews, makes explicit key events and relationships, and explains vocabulary, concepts, and references. Students demonstrate their knowledge through guided notes, graphic organizers, self-reflections, and visual representations. Tameka offers options for large projects, such as a dramatization, essay (with speech to text software), poster, or webpage, and allows students to work independently or in small groups. She explicitly states the grading criteria, assists the students in setting goals, and reviews her expectations for the students and classroom behavior.

Tameka works hard to provide supports that will allow all students to be successful. She teaches literacy by engaging her students in a love of books and circumvents barriers in reading, fluency, and writing, which often prevents students from participating and being successful. When asked how to teach all students successfully, she says, "let students know you care and provide clear communication and the necessary support for students to succeed. It takes time and effort to be a good teacher, but it is worth it."

Each of these principles helps students access and comprehend material, demonstrate knowledge, and facilitate active engagement in the learning process. UDL is not intended to make lessons or objectives easier. It supports all learners by acknowledging differences in learning, skill development, and interests. UDL requires teachers to intentionally provide a variety of supports so all students have the resources to overcome their barriers and learn (CAST, 2018).

Readers are *strongly encouraged* to visit the UDL website (www.udlguidelines.cast.org) to review the three principles and various checkpoints.

Direct instruction, sheltered instruction, and UDL are teaching methodologies designed to meet all students' needs, including those with disabilities. Incorporating these practices into daily teaching fosters an inclusive environment where all students have the necessary support to be successful. These three methodologies can be used in combination as well.

Comprehension Check

1   What are the steps of direct instruction?
2   How does sheltered instruction differ from direct instruction?
3   What are the three main principles of UDL?

Accommodations and Modifications

Teaching methodologies such as direct and sheltered instruction and UDL are foundational for effective instruction, but at times accommodations and modifications may be necessary. Students with special needs may require additional support through accommodations and modifications as identified on their IEPs, or as identified on their 504 plan, to provide their free and appropriate education.

Accommodations

Accommodations are supports given to an individual, group, or entire class designed to compensate for academic or behavioral challenges. While the rigor and expectations of the general education curriculum are not changed, accommodations assist students in accessing information and demonstrating their knowledge. They are incorporated into instructional methodologies to help "level the playing field" and give all students a fair opportunity for success.

There are four types of accommodations: presentation, response, setting, and timing. *Presentation accommodations*, such as audiobooks, text to speech, and graphic organizers, impact how the material is presented. They support students' ability to access and acquire information by circumventing areas of difficulty, such as reading, organizing, and processing information. For example, presenting directions both in writing and orally is an accommodation that allows students different means to access and comprehend that material. They can both hear it and read it. This accommodation does not make the assignment easier but provides additional supports to help the student understand the information.

The use of calculators, speech to text, and scribes are examples of *response accommodations*. They allow students to respond to or demonstrate knowledge by avoiding barriers in areas like memorization and fine motor skills. For instance, the use of multiplication charts for long division requires students to know the steps and process of division but supports deficits in memorizing multiplication facts. Students must still know how to divide but may not be successful in demonstrating their knowledge without the accommodation due to difficulties with memorization rather than a failure to understand division.

Setting accommodations permit the use of small group environments or preferential seating within a classroom. These changes in setting work to mitigate distractions and help students focus, provide behavioral support, and address students' physical challenges. They allow a student with limited mobility a desk near the door, a student with ADHD a testing environment with fewer distractions, and a student who is hard of hearing a seat at the front of the class. These accommodations provide students with the environmental support necessary to learn and participate in school.

In some instances, *timing accommodations* are provided in terms of scheduling, additional time, and breaks. Timing accommodations align crucial assessments or instruction to particular times of the day (for instance, in the morning or right after lunch) to when the student performs better. For example, critical assessments may be conducted after lunch when the student is best able to concentrate, thus ensuring more valid results. Students may be given extra time to complete assignments or assessments to compensate for difficulties focusing or processing information. More frequent work breaks may be afforded to students who tire easily or need a respite. These accommodations adjust the timing of events to allow students to perform without lowering academic or behavioral requirements while avoiding barriers and capitalizing on students' strengths.

Some states combined *timing* and *setting* accommodations into one category (*timing/setting*). The individual accommodations remain the same but the classifications themselves maybe combined.

Accommodations do not lower expectations but provide the necessary supports to help students succeed. While they are often integrated into lessons and granted to the entire class, students with disabilities may have specific accommodations documented on their IEPs or 504 Plan. For example, a student may have an accommodation to have a peer note-taker, but an individual teacher could also provide the entire class an outline or guided notes. Outlines and guided notes facilitate comprehension and allow students to focus on lectures, discussions, and activities more than on taking notes. Documentation ensures the availability of the accommodation rather than relying on the methodology of a teacher.

IEPs

IEPs, discussed in depth in Chapter 5, document a student's accommodations for testing and classroom purposes. IDEA mandates that students with disabilities participate in state- and district-wide assessments and may be provided testing accommodations when doing so. The vast majority of students with disabilities are administered the same grade level (not ability level) state- and district-wide assessments as their general education peers. It is important to note that a tiny percentage of students with the most severe disabilities receive an alternate assessment, rather than the standard form of these assessments. The vast majority of students with disabilities, though, take the same assessments as their general education peers to measure their grade level proficiency and academic progress. For these students, their IEP team may determine that testing accommodations are necessary to facilitate their performance. Each state has its policies on what constitutes an allowable (okay to use) or not allowable (not okay to use) testing accommodation. Testing accommodations should only be provided if documented on an IEP or 504 Plan and aligned to state requirements. Additionally, even though the accommodations are documented for state- and district-wide assessments, they should be made available for all testing situations (for instance, quizzes, chapter tests) as classroom accommodations. These accommodations do not change the content of the assessments but provide supports for presentation, response, setting, and time (University of Kansas, n.d.).

Classroom accommodations are those provided to the student on a regular ongoing basis. They may be used for both behavioral and academic content to help "level the playing field" in the classroom. These are often the same accommodations as those for state- and district-wide testing, but there may be some differences. Typically, any testing accommodation a student receives should also be provided as a classroom accommodation. Classroom accommodations are determined by the student's IEP team and documented on their IEP. If accommodations are documented on an IEP, they must be made available to the student.

504 Plans

Section 504 of the Rehabilitation Act, as discussed in Chapter 1, is a civil rights law that guarantees reasonable accommodations from any organization that receives federal funding for any person with a known or perceived disability. This law applies to most schools since the vast majority receive federal funding. Section 504 differs from IDEA in its definition of a disability and the assurances provided for academic and behavioral support. As discussed in Chapters 1 and 4, IDEA clearly defines specific eligibility criteria for special education, while Section 504 has a much broader definition of what constitutes a disability. Therefore, a student may receive supports through Section 504, who would not otherwise qualify under IDEA. The supports provided by Section 504 are reasonable accommodations (not necessarily specially designed instruction or special education services) as defined on the student's 504, also referred to as an Individualized Accommodation Plan. See Table 6.1 for a comparison of the difference between a 504 Plan and an IEP.

Students qualify for a 504 Plan if they have a disability or a physical or mental impairment that substantially limits one or more major life activities. Determining eligibility and reasonable academic or behavioral accommodations for a 504 Plan is typically done by a multidisciplinary team consisting of both general and special education teachers, the student's parents, a school administrator, and possibly the students themselves.

While the components of an IEP are federally mandated, those of a 504 Plan are not and may look different depending on the state, district, and school. These plans should include the student's strengths, areas of need, and the reasonable accommodations provided to address those needs (DREDF, n.d.; Lawless Frank, Christman, Baldwin & Richards, 2019; Skalski & Stanek, 2010; Stanberry, 2014). For instance, the team

Table 6.1 504 Plan vs. IEP

	504 Plan	Individualized Education Program (IEP)
Law	Section 504 of the Rehabilitation Act	Individuals with Disabilities Education Improvement Act (IDEA)
Disability	a physical or mental impairment which substantially limits one or more major life activities	Identifies 13 disabilities categories with defined eligibility requirements
Documents	Reasonable accommodations	Free and appropriate public education, including: • Individualized instructions • Related services • Transportation • Extended school year • Accommodations • Modified and functional curriculum • Annual goals and objectives • Transition services

may determine that a student with ADHD (a mental impairment that impacts one or more major life activities) has behaviors that interfere with their learning and needs reasonable accommodations for extended time on assessments and assistive technology for writing. These accommodations are documented on the 504 Plan and implemented in both the classroom and testing situations. See Table 6.2 for a sample 504 Plan.

504 Plans typically provide reasonable accommodations rather than modifications or related services that may be provided through an IEP.

Table 6.2 Sample 504 Plan

J.C. Barrett Elementary School

Date of plan: **Date of next review:**

Student's name: Christian Murray   **Date of birth:**   **Grade:**

Parents/guardians: Juan and Maria Murray

Eligibility: Christian has been diagnosed with ADHD, which impacts his ability to organize materials and complete assignments on time.

Student's areas of strength:
Christian is outgoing and energetic. He excels in art and drawing anime. He is intelligent and a creative problem solver.

Description of eligibility determination and need:
Christian has difficulties with his time management and organization. He has multiple late and missing assignments and has trouble organizing and keeping track of his materials and assignments.

(continued)

Table 6.2 (continued)

Area of Need	Accommodations	Responsible Party	Allowable for State/District Testing
Time Management	Extended time of tests	Special education teachers	yes
	Small group (fewer distractions) for testing	Special education teacher	yes
Organization	Providing a checklist of materials needed for class	General Education teacher	Not applicable
	Teacher supervision in writing down assignments	General Education teacher	Not applicable

Source: Lawless Frank, Christman, Baldwin, & Richards, 2019.

Modifications

Modifications change the assessment, curriculum, or learning objectives in some manner. These changes impact and lower the rigor, expectations, or requirements for learning. With modifications, students typically are not expected to achieve at the same levels as their general education peers. Modifications may be made within the general education curriculum standards or result in the use of alternate academic standards for instruction. These changes may mean that the student has fewer options on a multiple-choice test or a shorter essay to write. It could also mean different curriculum (basic or functional mathematics rather than algebra) or instructional materials (lower reading level). Decisions to offer modifications are determined by the student's IEP team and are not allowable for standardized or formal assessments such as state- and district-wide tests. Typically, students are required to take all parts of their grade level (not ability level) state- and district-wide assessments without any changes to the actual test. Therefore, students may take alternate assessments when modifications substantially impact the student's access and learning in the college and career readiness standards. It is worth noting that alternate assessment results are still included in a school's and district's overall achievement test results and any "report cards" a state may publish based on those results.

Modifications can include a different curriculum entirely, such as community-based instruction and functional skills. This alternative curriculum is more common for students with moderate to severe disabilities in middle and high school who take those alternate state- and district-wide assessments. Alternate standards-based curricula are typically offered in special education classrooms and focus on providing the student with the skills necessary for transitioning into adulthood and include those essential for career readiness and independent living. As students grow older, moving instruction into actual community settings (e.g., at a grocery store, at a worksite) still provides for inclusion with people without disabilities, albeit not in general education classrooms.

6.2 Case Study Accommodation vs. Modification

Identify each of the following as an accommodation or a modification and justify your answer.

1 Providing Steve a scribe when writing an essay on the causes of the civil war.
2 Allowing Tamara to skip a portion of an assignment and focus on crucial information.
3 Reading a history test aloud to Rita while the rest of the class reads it silently.
4 Reducing the number of options on a multiple-choice test for Zac.
5 Checking in with Monica at the end of the school day to ensure she has all her homework assignments written in her daily planner.
6 Allowing Raul twice as long to complete a literature comprehension test.
7 Permitting Yosef to reference an addition chart for a two-digit addition math assignment on carrying.
8 The use of a spell checker for Jorge when writing a narrative poem.
9 Providing Ashley with a fidget tool during classroom lectures and assessments.
10 Highlighting keywords in word problems for Nick in math class.

Students with disabilities should be provided the least intrusive interventions necessary for success and educated as similarly to their general education peers as possible. If and when additional academic and behavioral supports are required, the accommodations should least alter the presentation, response, setting, or timing expectations provided to general education peers. For instance, preferential seating near a teacher should be tried before an alternative environment for a student with behavior problems. While modifications are necessary for some instances, accommodations should always be tried first. Remember, the principle of LRE states all students with disabilities should be educated with peers without disabilities to the maximum extent *appropriate* as determined by IEP teams. IEP teams almost always include general education teachers who can assist the team in considering the LRE.

Comprehension Check

1 What is the difference between an accommodation and a modification?
2 Identify the four types of accommodations.
3 Why should the least intrusive interventions be tried first in supporting students with disabilities?

Additional Instructional Considerations

Some teaching components are partially beneficial for all students, especially those with disabilities and other diverse learning needs that can be embedded into UDL, shelter and direct instruction, or any instructional pedagogy. These include data-driven instruction, providing specific student feedback and developing appropriate and caring relationships with students. They are the foundation for effective teaching regardless of the students, pedagogy, method, or curriculum.

Data-driven Instruction

Data-driven instruction aligns teaching to the needs of an individual, group, or entire class. This process uses a cycle of assessment, analysis, and decision making to make informed instructional choices. The data sources used can be formative and summative assessments, which are beneficial for guiding daily and long-term instruction. For instance, an exit slip assessment given at the end of the class provides a check for what the students understood and where they need additional assistance. This information is analyzed and incorporated into the following day's lesson to clarify concepts, provide positive feedback on what the students have done well or mastered, and guide the lesson's direction. This process provides both the teacher and students with a clear understanding of what they know and do not know.

A pretest at the beginning of a unit can provide a baseline of what the students already know. This information is analyzed and used to determine the unit's direction while emphasizing the content that needs more attention. Observations on classroom behaviors (a formative assessment) can provide daily insight into the adjustments needed in teaching or management strategies, and provide required measurable data. Using data to inform instructions productively directs the teacher's energy and ensures students learn key concepts and ideas. Summative assessments can be used to compare pretest to posttest results to check both individual student and group achievement and assist in long-term instructional planning.

Specific Feedback

Providing clear feedback on an individual's academic and behavioral strengths and areas of need provides students with direct insight into their own performances. The more specific the feedback (both positive and corrective), the higher the potential benefit to and subsequent progress of the student. For example, identifying what the student is doing correctly in a math problem and where mistakes are occurring provides greater insight than merely marking the question right or wrong. By the teacher specifically informing the student as to what they are doing correctly and incorrectly, it allows students to ask questions, clarify information and directions, and focus on areas where mistakes are occurring. For example, if a student receives a 70% on a writing assignment with little or no specific information on what they did correctly in terms of content, grammar, and structure, it is difficult for them to develop an appropriate strategy for improvement. Was the poor grade due to problems with verb tense? Failure to follow the directions? Word choices? Choppiness or disjointed writing? Without this specific information, students are unsure of what they are doing correctly or incorrectly.

Specific feedback is useful for both academics and behaviors. It is particularly important, especially for behaviors, to focus on the positive and what the student is doing correctly ("Shawn, thank you for walking into the classroom quietly."). Positive feedback provides the student with attention and acknowledgment of what they are doing right. It clarifies the teacher's expectations and may subvert students' attempts to gain teacher attention for inappropriate behavior. Teachers should identify a minimum of four positive student behaviors for every one negative comment. Positive attention or praise is both a good proactive and reactive strategy. When it becomes necessary to provide critical feedback, it should be specific and focus on the student's behavior rather than subjective or personal. For example, it is better to say to Shawn on a different day, "Your talking is disruptive to the rest of the class" versus "Shawn, I don't want what to deal with you today. You are a constant troublemaker."

When a student demonstrates perseverance, it is especially important to provide positive feedback. Praising perseverance acknowledges the student's struggles and recognizes their commitment to learning, and encourages continued persistence ("Antonio, I know this is difficult, but I like how you keep working at it"). Perseverance and the ability to keep trying should be viewed as being equally important, if not more so, than getting the correct answers. Students who develop perseverance also tend to be higher achievers and build self-confidence in their own abilities to succeed.

Teachers must provide students with encouragement and opportunities to apply feedback. The feedback alone may have little impact without continuing opportunities to use it. Applying feedback may mean that the teacher conferences with the student to discuss their performance and how to improve. Students may be asked to rewrite or revise assignments, write reflections, practice performing a behavior correctly, or review prior feedback before beginning a task. Providing a means to learn from and apply the feedback is critical to maximizing its benefits.

Relationship Building

The importance of developing appropriate relationships in school cannot be overstated. Quality relationships are paramount to effective teaching and behavior management. The relationships among teachers, students, and peers form the basis of an inclusive classroom community. The most important of these is the relationship between the teacher and the individual student and is an essential ingredient in effective behavior management (Wang, Haertel, & Walberg, 1993). Students perform and behave in class, at least in part, based on their perception of their relationships with the teacher. Individual students need to feel this connection to progress towards their academic and behavioral potential. Students put more effort into classes where they perceive a positive, caring relationship with the teacher (Weinstein, Tomlinson-Clarke, & Curran, 2004). When students do make errors academically and behaviorally, they are more likely to respond to corrective feedback when they trust the teacher and believe the teacher has their best interests at heart.

A student's knowledge and use of social skills can play a critical role in developing these relationships. Teachers often find it easier to establish a connection with students who know and employ appropriate interpersonal and relationship skills. Students with disabilities may struggle with this, impacting their ability to form relationships with teachers and peers. Recall, students with disabilities may have difficulties in processing what others say (e.g., slow to respond to directions), expressing themselves to others (e.g., unclear message invoking frustration on the listener's part) or in pragmatics (e.g., talking to the teacher as if they were neighborhood friends). Students with speech and language disorders and other disabilities, may struggle with social issues and isolation among their peers, making a quality relationship with teachers even more imperative. Social skills will be further discussed in Chapter 8.

Comprehension Check

1   How is data used to drive instructions?
2   Why is providing positive feedback valuable?
3   What are the benefits of developing a quality relationship with students?

References

CAST (2018). Universal Design for Learning Guidelines version 2.2. Retrieved from http://udlguidelines.cast.org.

Disability Rights Education & Defense Fund (DREDF). (n.d.). A comparison of ADA, IDEA, and Section 504. Retrieved from http://dredf.org/advocacy/comparison.html.

Gersten, R., Woodward, J., & Darch, C. (1986). Direct instruction: A research-based approach to curriculum design and teaching. *Exceptional Children*, 53(1), 17–31.

Iris Center. (2011). *Teaching English Language Learners: Effective Instructional Practices*. Retrieved from https://iris.peabody.vanderbilt.edu/module/ell.

Lawless Frank, C., Christman, J.T., Baldwin, J.L., & Richards, S.B. (2019). *Managing Classroom and Student Behavior*. New York, NY: Routledge.

Skalski, A.K., & Stanek, J. (2010). Section 504: A guide for parents and educators. Bethesda, MD. National Association of School Psychologists. Retrieved from www.bpsd.org/Downloads/Section%20504.pdf.

Stanberry, K. (2014). *Understanding 504 plans*. Retrieved from www.understood.org/en/school-learning/special-services/504-plan/understanding-504-plans.

Universal Design for Learning Guidelines. Retrieved from http://udlguidelines.cast.org, 06/2020.

University of Kansas. (n.d.). Assessment accommodations. Retrieved from www.specialconnections.ku.edu/~kucrl/cgi-bin/drupal/?q=assessment/assessment_accommodations, 06/2020.

Wang, M. C., Haertel, G. D., & Walberg, H. J. (1993). Toward a knowledge base for school learning. *Review of Educational Research*, 63(3), 249–294.

Weinstein, C., Tomlinson-Clarke, S., & Curran, M. (2004). Toward a conception of culturally responsive classroom management. *Journal of Teacher Education*, 55(1), 25–38.

7 Collaboration and Co-Teaching

Catherine Lawless Frank

Objectives: After reading this chapter, students will be able to:

1 Explain the difference between collaboration and consultation
2 Describe the six models of co-teaching
3 Identify barriers to collaboration and ways to overcome challenges
4 Identify best practices in collaborating with parents.

The Least Restrictive Environment (LRE) provision under IDEA requires all students with disabilities to be educated alongside their non-disabled peers to the maximum extent appropriate. LRE has resulted in approximately 80% of students with disabilities being educated at least 40% of the school day in the general education classroom (National Center for Education Statistics, 2019). While collaboration has always been an ingredient to effective education, the realities of LRE make it essential. In schools, collaboration takes many forms, such as grade or curriculum teams, IEP teams, assessment teams, and co-teaching. Some are mandated by laws such as IEP teams, while others support best practices like grade-level teams and co-teaching. General education teachers participate in special education teams to determine student eligibility, IEP teams to help establish and implement goals, progress monitoring or data teams to track student progress, as well as co-teaching and collaborating with related services personnel.

Collaboration is a form of professional development essential to supporting teachers and meeting the needs of all students, including those with disabilities. It is a goal-oriented process in which two or more individuals work together to complete a task or solve a problem. It goes beyond cooperation to involve work jointly executed with a shared vision. Each person brings knowledge and expertise to form a partnership with a common goal (Moseley, n.d.).

An effective collaborative process involves clearly defining the goal or purpose of the partnership. For example, the goal may be to determine the necessary specially designed instruction, most appropriate LRE, or a co-teaching approach that best supports all students. A clear goal provides all partners with a path to focus and direct energies and available resources. The clearer the goal, the easier it is to supply that direction. A brainstorming session then occurs to determine and document potential solutions or ways to achieve the goal. The team then decides which plan or idea to implement based on the target, needs, and available resources. As implementation occurs, progress is evaluated on an ongoing basis. Revisions are made as necessary, and implementation and reevaluation continue until the goal is achieved.

Collaboration vs. Consultation

There is a difference between collaboration and consultation. Consultation involves a problem-solving team, which may include teachers, parents, administrators, and experts in the field that share knowledge, brainstorm ideas, and design potential solutions to an academic or behavioral concern. Teachers then implement these ideas and possible solutions within their classrooms and report back to the team about their effectiveness. If the area of concern is mitigated, then the consultation process ends. If it is not, then the team reconvenes to continue devising solutions. The majority of team members work to design solutions but are not involved in implementation. There is joint work in devising potential solutions but not in the execution.

Consolation can happen at both a formal and informal level. A formal approach often involves a consultant, such as a behavioral consultant or a school team of consultants (e.g., Intervention Assistance Team) that share their expertise and help design solutions for academic or behavioral concerns. Much more common though is informal consultation between colleagues. Teachers often work as consultants for each other to offer advice, brainstorm solutions, and share insights and strategies. This approach to professional development happens in meetings, hallways, faculty lounges, and throughout the school building and day. While it is often not a formalized process (although it can be), this sharing of knowledge and resources is an invaluable support to colleagues, students, and parents (Richards, Lawless Frank, Sableski, & Arnold, 2016).

Comprehension Check

1   Identify the differences between a consultation and a collaboration.
2   How can collaboration and consolation be used as professional development?
3   What is the difference between formal and informal consolation?

Co-Teaching

Co-teaching requires considerable collaborative investment and helps provide students the academic and behavioral support necessary to learn and participate in school. Legislative reforms, such as IDEA's Least Restrictive Environment principle, support co-teaching as it facilitates educating students with special needs alongside their nondisabled peers in a general education classroom. It involves two equal professionals (rather than a teacher and a paraprofessional) in the same space, working together to educate all students. In this environment, there should not be a distinction between special education and general education but an inclusive atmosphere where both teachers are responsible for all students (Hanover, 2012). This approach reduces the stigma of a special education label and encourages high expectations with an emphasis on career and college readiness skills. Though initially developed to support students with disabilities, co-teaching allows both professionals to work together to contribute knowledge, skills, and resources to better the outcome for the entire class (Graziano & Navarrete, 2012; Magiera, Smith, Zigmond & Gebauer, 2005; Murawski & Dieker, 2004).

Successful and productive co-teaching does not happen by chance and requires administrative support for the staffing, resources, and time necessary to jointly plan and implement lessons, as well as organizing shared space, ideas, resources, materials, management, and strategies. It is a partnership that necessitates willingness, compromise, flexibility, and perseverance (Brown, Howerter & Morgan, 2013; Mastropieri, Scruggs, Graetz, Norland, Gardizi & McDuffie, 2005; Richards, et al., 2016). Effective implementation takes time and effort, but it can facilitate growth in students and teachers alike when done well. Students benefit from increased individualized attention and differing teacher personalities and instructional styles, which may better align with diverse needs. It can allow for more innovative instructional practices as educators brainstorm and work together to develop and implement lessons. Social skills can be enhanced as teachers model appropriate interactions, respectful partnerships, and collaborative skills that enable teachable moments on cooperation, compromise, and handling disagreements. Co-teaching can also serve as a support system and a form of professional development for teachers as they learn from and support each other (Kaplan, 2012).

Co-teaching is a commitment, similar to parenting, that requires a partnership built on clear communication and mutual respect. It works best if it is voluntary with a compatible partner rather than mandated, particularly if the administrative mandate does little more than assign partners. Forming a successful co-working relationship takes time, commitment, and compromise. This dedication is necessary for the joint decision making required to ensure both teachers agree with the classroom structure, philosophy, expectations, and the multitude of other decisions necessary for collaboratively supporting the diverse needs of students. Compromise is needed, and while both partners do not have to agree on every decision, they must present a united front to the students. Without this cohesive teacher presence, students lack clear guidance and understanding of the structure and boundaries resulting in confusion and potential behavioral issues (Murawski, 2019).

Co-teaching involves two professionals, and students should view both as equally responsible for the academic and behavioral well-being of all students (Murawski, 2019). The teacher and paraprofessional's relationship, by definition, involves an imbalance of power (the teacher is typically "in charge"), which is less conducive to a co-teaching relationship. While co-teaching is often viewed as involving general and special education teachers, it can comprise other professionals, such as related services personnel, English language teachers, and curriculum support staff. This partnership can be for a single class period (such as English language arts) or throughout the entire school day.

A key to successful co-teaching is that instruction is mutually planned, delivered, and assessed, requiring both professionals to be equal partners. It can be misconstrued as being one professional as the primary instructor and the other assisting or observing in the classroom. The overuse of this approach is a misrepresentation of the intent of co-teaching and limits its potential benefits. There are, in fact, six different models or configurations of co-teaching. No one model is the right approach for all situations. Factors such as lesson objectives, content, student population, and needed supports for students should play a role in determining the best strategy while ensuring variation in the co-teaching models used (Friend & Cook, 2000; Richards et al., 2016; Witcher & Feng, 2010).

Models of Co-Teaching

One Teach, One Observe

Figure 7.1 includes a diagram illustrating the most basic co-teaching model, one teach-one observe.

In this approach, one professional is the primary instructor for the lesson while the second professional observes either a student(s), the class, or the co-teacher (Friend & Cook, 2000). This approach is used as needed to (1) gather data or (2) provide professional development.

For instance, while the lesson is being conducted by the first professional, the second professional may observe a particular student to progress monitor an IEP goal or examine behaviors such as the amount of time on task. The second professional may assess the class's overall behavior, social dynamics, or levels of interest or engagement. This approach may be used as a form of requested professional development. The second professional observes the first conduct a lesson and provides constructive feedback on program fidelity, insights into what is working, and suggestions for improvement. Professional development and giving feedback should only be conducted as requested and agreed upon by both professionals. The roles of both the primary instructor and

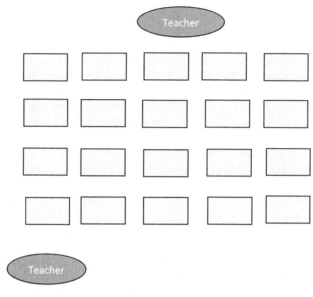

Figure 7.1 Co-Teaching – One Teach, One Observe

observer should rotate and be utilized on occasion by both teachers. One professional should not always be the lead teacher and the other always the observer. The *one teach, one observe* approach should not be a primary means of co-teaching but used as necessary to gather data or enhance professional development (Friend & Cook, 2000; Richards, et al., 2016).

One Teach, One Assist

Figure 7.2 illustrates the one teach–one assist model.

One professional is the primary instructor, while the other provides student support in the *one teach, one assist* model (Friend & Cook, 2000). Here one professional is available to offer assistance to individuals or groups of students while the other is providing whole-class instruction. This approach facilitates academic or behavioral interventions by clarifying content, ensuring students are on task, and intervening in behavioral concerns. This approach, however, may also be overused as the primary means of co-teaching. When used extensively, co-teaching benefits are minimized, especially if one professional is always the primary instructor while the other assumes the role of "assistant." In upper grades, one professional tends to have more content knowledge, and this approach can create an imbalance of both power and responsibilities rather than a true partnership. Overuse may inhibit collaboration, co-planning, open communication, and lead students to see one professional as having more authority within the classroom. It can be particularly problematic if the

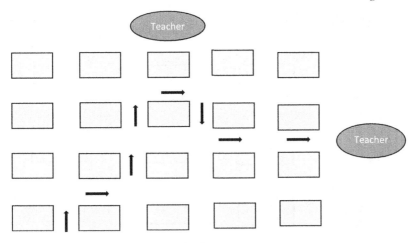

Figure 7.2 Co-Teaching – One Teach, One Assist

primary instructor is always the general education teacher and the special education teacher assists. This imbalance may lead both the teachers and the students to view the special education teacher as there to assist only the IEP students. To maximize co-teaching benefits, the *one teach, one assist* model should be used judiciously with each partner assuming the roles and responsibilities of assisting and teaching. All co-teaching approaches are beneficial, but no one model should be the sole or dominant means of instruction (Friend & Cook, 2000; Richards, et al., 2016).

Parallel Teaching

Figure 7.3 includes an illustration of the parallel teaching model.

Parallel teaching is a regrouping method in which the co-teachers divide the class into halves. Each professional is then responsible for teaching the same lesson to their half of the students (Friend & Cook, 2000). The lesson content and teaching responsibilities are the same for both partners, but the student to teacher ratio is smaller, allowing for more individual support and feedback throughout the lesson. This approach can be used to introduce and teach a new math topic, model a science experiment, debate social studies or history topics, discuss a reading, preview a project or writing assignment, or review information for a test or quiz. The information and instruction provided to both groups remain the same, while the smaller numbers allow for more student interaction and responsiveness to students' needs. Additionally, halving the class enables the teachers to assign students to groups for various reasons. It allows for separating students who are disruptive when together,

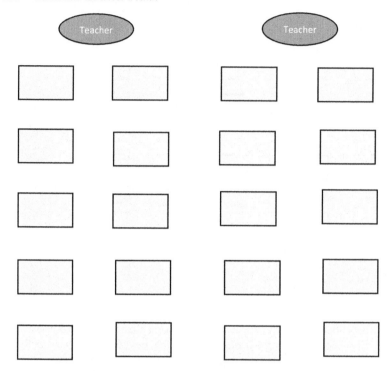

Figure 7.3 Co-Teaching – Parallel Teaching

balancing the number of students in need of extra support or the amount of high achieving students who can contribute to their peers' learning.

In this approach, both professionals are equal partners with shared responsibilities towards planning, teaching, and assessing instruction (Friend & Cook, 2000; Richards, et al., 2016).

Station Teaching

Figure 7.4 illustrates the station teaching model.

Station teaching requires each professional to teach different content. Students are divided into three or four smaller groups and rotate through different unique learning stations.

For example, in an elementary class, the co-teachers could have students working on the addition of 1-digit numbers for practice and 2-digit numbers as a new topic. The co-teachers divide the class into three groups and create three stations. The first station introduces 2-digit addition using manipulatives and is taught by one of the co-teachers. The second station introduces 2-digit addition through written problems and is taught by the second co-teacher. The third station involves

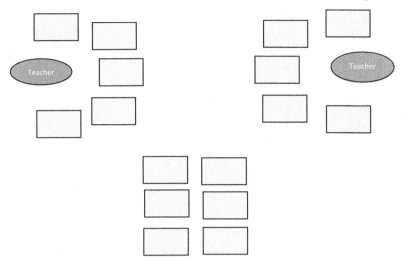

Figure 7.4 Co-Teaching – Station Teaching

independent practice on a skill the students have recently mastered, such as 1-digit addition. Each small group of students would spend a designated amount of time in each station, and both professionals would teach all students. Since both professionals are engaged in teaching other students, it is important to ensure the third group has a clear understanding of the assignment, expectations, and procedures (such as how and when to ask a question) at the independent practice station. This approach demonstrates an equal partnership among professionals. It requires collaborative planning for the stations and clear communication as to the structure and expectations (how do the groups rotate, how much time in each station, who will monitor the independent work station) (Friend & Cook, 2000; Richards, et al., 2016).

Alternative Teaching

Figure 7.5 includes an illustration of the alternative teaching model.

At times, it will be necessary to teach different content to different groups of students within the same classroom. This approach is *alternative teaching*. Here students are regrouped, typically based on their needs, with each professional teaching different content to a group. For instance, based on the results of a science test, one professional may work with a small group of students to re-teach critical concepts while the other provides instruction to the rest of the class. One group may be provided enrichment while the other group continues to receive the essential teaching, or one group may be students who were absent during the crucial instruction. It can be used to pre-teach a new concept or skill

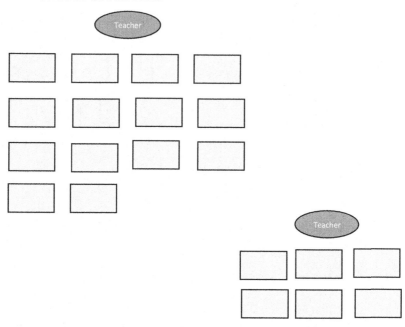

Figure 7.5 Co-Teaching – Alternative Teaching

to a group that needs extra attention in understanding the vocabulary and academic language for the next lesson or unit. The professionals are still responsible for co-planning, but different instruction is provided to the different groups. In this approach, the student grouping (who is in each group) and instructor role (teaching a small group vs. large group) should vary. The groups should be fluid based on needs, and the professionals should rotate instructional groups demonstrating an equal responsibility for all students (Friend & Cook, 2000; Richards, et al., 2016).

Team Teaching

Figure 7.6 includes an illustration of the team teaching model.

In *team teaching*, both professionals are responsible for delivering the same content to the same students at the same time in the same classroom. This approach is a true partnership in which both instructors work to build and teach lessons to all students, both general and special education. Both professionals are equally responsible for teaching, managing, and assessing students. One excellent use of this model discussed in Chapter 8 is having one co-teacher delivering content while the other co-teacher models executive functions, learning strategies, and/or metacognitive skills. Chapter 8 outlines how co-teachers can teach academic content standards and the skills necessary for students to become more productive and independent learners. Teachers in this approach

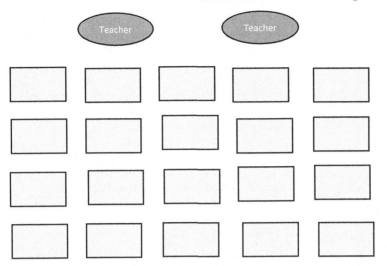

Figure 7.6 Co-Teaching – Team Teaching

must have a shared vision and practice clear open communication as it requires the most collaboration and cohesion of the co-teaching models (Friend & Cook, 2000; Richards, et al., 2016).

Case Study 7.1 Co-Teaching Models

Mr. Rubicon and Mrs. Mathis are special and general education teachers that co-teach together. In a joint planning session, they decided to teach the following content standard next week:

Write informative/explanatory texts, including the narration of historical events, scientific procedures/experiments, or technical processes.

1   Design two different lessons using a different co-teaching strategy for each
2   Determine who will be responsible for each aspect of the lesson.

The six models of co-teaching offer variety for professionals to collaboratively work together to teach all students. No one model is the correct approach in all circumstances, nor should one be the sole means of co-teaching (especially *one teach, one observe*, and *one teach, one assist*). Commitment from the administration is vital for co-teaching as well as mutual respect and clear open communication between partners. Time must be dedicated to joint planning and revisiting and reevaluating what is working and what is not working for both the students and individual partners (Murawski, 2019).

It is also worth noting that these models are not "pure," that is, co-teachers do not have to choose between one or another for a lesson.

They could begin team teaching and shift to station teaching, parallel teaching, or alternative teaching within the same lesson. One important caveat is that co-teachers need to teach students the logistics of getting into groups, going to their assigned stations, or with their assigned co-teacher. This procedural instruction saves time and confusion and is absolutely necessary for a co-teaching environment.

Comprehension Check

1   What are the essential components of successful co-teaching?
2   Identify the six models of co-teaching.
3   How can co-teaching be used for both professional development and improving student outcomes?

Barriers and Overcoming Challenges

The process of collaboration and co-teaching requires two or more people to work together, resulting in potential complications and obstacles. Success is not guaranteed. Co-teaching requires time, energy, and compromise while adapting to the trials of joint problem-solving and instruction. A shortage of resources, differing perspectives, beliefs, and interpersonal skills can confound the partnership, potentially making a compromise and consensus-building a challenge. Barriers to this process can be pragmatic, philosophical, or psychological and require a willingness, flexibility, determination, and planning to overcome.

Pragmatic barriers are logistical such as resources and time, and practical such as administrative support, funding, and competing responsibilities. Overcoming these barriers often requires prioritizing and advocacy on the part of co-teachers and administrators. The necessary resources, time, and personnel must be committed to collaborative projects, especially co-teaching, for these endeavors to be productive. Securing commitments may involve advocating for students' and teachers' needs and prioritizing resources to get the most "bang for the buck." Priority must be given to scheduling shared planning and work times, adjusting responsibilities, and funding for professional development and training. While some of these barriers may be circumvented without administrative support, such as planning before or after school, advocating for and gaining the necessary commitments is often critical for long-term collaborative success (Richards, et al., 2016; Taylor, Smiley, & Richards, 2015; Welch, 2000).

Other types of barriers are more psychological and philosophical. These barriers stem from an individual's beliefs about roles and responsibilities and a willingness to compromise and change. A person's position or, more importantly, their views about their role within a classroom or school may pose a barrier as work requirements are redefined, and responsibilities are adjusted. This transformation of work requirements may challenge a person's concept of their purpose within a school, teaching philosophy, and corresponding duties. For example, a teacher who has taught biology for ten years and then is asked to co-teach with a special education teacher may struggle with redefining their roles and responsibilities within the classroom. Over those ten years, the biology teacher has developed a teaching philosophy, style, and a protocol for instruction. The special education teacher, in contrast, has taught in a resource room and is unsure of how successful co-teaching in the general education class might be. Both may struggle to readjust their views and question their ability to collaborate with a person with a different skill set, knowledge base, and perceptions about teaching. Case Study 7.2 will challenge you to think about collaboration.

Case Study 7.2 Co-Teaching: Developing Relationships

Ms. Jaidyn Lisset, a first-year teacher, was hired into a co-teaching position at the Rocky Fork Community School. She is excited about her job but wishes she had a couple of years of experience to "find her footing" before being asked to co-teach. Her co-teacher, Mrs. Christina Joseph, is a special education instructor who has taught in the district for eight years and is well loved and respected by her students. Jaidyn met Christina during her interview process but did not feel the instant connection and friendship she had hoped to find. When she envisioned co-teaching, she imagined the great relationship and camaraderie they would develop rather than the challenges of starting and establishing a new partnership. The newness of this situation has led Ms. Lisset to feel tense, nervous, and insecure about beginning her first year teaching.

What could Jaidyn do to begin developing a collaborative partnership with Christina?

What potential challenges will Christina and Jaidyn face?

Jaidyn is a novice teacher, while Christina has years of experience, creating a disparity in professional knowledge. What advice would you give Jaidyn about establishing herself as a novice yet equal partner in the co-teaching relationship?

These struggles exist throughout collaborative relationships, such as with a beginning general education teacher assigned to co-teach with an experienced special education teacher. The novice teacher may have envisioned what their classroom would look and be like and developed a sense of ownership towards "their" students. They may feel intimidated by an experienced teacher, question their own level of expertise, and be conflicted about co-teaching and sharing their space with another instructor. Or, imagine two teachers with differing approaches to class-room and behavior management navigating the consistent enforcement of rules and expectations. Developing a respectful relationship between partners, adjusting one's belief about roles, respecting professional differences, and having a willingness to compromise is essential for successful collaboration. Collaboration and co-teaching can be challenging and often requires examining the situation from a different perspective and seeing another's point of view (Richards, et al., 2016).

A key to effective collaboration is clear communication, but things go awry even with the best intentions. Collaboration may sound ideal in concept, but challenges and disagreements do occur. These conflicts can be useful when dealt with openly, professionally, and with a willingness to compromise, but conflicts can be detrimental when unresolved. Conflicts can help to clarify situations, bridge cultural divides, and improve interpersonal skills. When conflicts do arise, it is imperative to revisit the goal, roles and responsibilities, and areas of agreement before defining areas of serious disagreement. Putting aside emotions, asking clarifying questions, and identifying commonalities can help clear up the misunderstanding and illuminate different perspectives. Collaboration is a give-and-take process requiring time and trust to build effective partnerships. While it does not require friendship, it does require respect for and among all partners. (Caspersen, 2014; Girard & Koch, 1996; Richards et al., 2016; Welch, 2000).

Comprehension Check

1   How do pragmatic barriers differ from philosophical and psychological ones?
2   Identify some practical steps for overcoming barriers.
3   In what ways can conflicts in the collaborative process be beneficial?

Collaborating with Parents

In special education, IDEA mandates a parent's rights to participate in determining eligibility and the design and implementation of their child's education program. This participation is necessary to develop appropriate IEP goals and determine the specially designed instruction essential for achieving those goals. Parents must receive reports of their child's course or content grades and their child's progress towards IEP goals and objectives. Parents are a key and integral part of special education, and it is vital to cultivate partnerships and working relationships to best meet the student's academic and behavioral needs.

It is a teacher's responsibility to initiate and foster positive parental partnerships. The same concepts for developing relationships with the parents of general education students also apply to the parents of special education students. Clear, open, and frequent communication that focuses on the positive aspects of the student's performance is especially important in working with parents of students with special needs. Frequently, conversations with schools can be focused on negative information (struggles with academics, failing grades, behavioral challenges), and highlighting the positive helps foster a collaborative relationship. No parent wants to hear "all the bad things" about their child. Such emphases in communication can breed apathy in the parents toward the school or even hostility among educators and parents.

Similar to collaboration within schools, pragmatic, philosophical, and psychological barriers impede developing meaningful partnerships with parents. Prioritizing the time and resources needed to commit to healthy and regular parent participation may pose challenges to schools, teachers, and parents alike. Disagreements may ensue about fundamental issues, such as what services a school should provide to ensure an appropriate education for a child. Other challenges can be logistical; parents' schedules may conflict with teachers' availability, making communication and/or conferences during a school day difficult. Problems may also exist in beliefs about roles, responsibilities, and parenting and teaching styles. The realities of teaching or parenting may not conform to the other's beliefs and expectations.

A teacher's view of a parent's role, parenting style, or what a parent should be doing may differ from reality ("If it were my kid …" or "Why don't the parents just …"). A parent's view of a teacher (or school's) role, teaching style, or what the teacher should be doing may also differ from reality ("The teacher should be …" "I don't understand why the school …"). These differing perspectives can make developing a working relationship challenging. Overcoming barriers requires clear, honest, and open communication, flexibility, and a willingness to acknowledge differing views.

At times, conflicts arise between parents and schools around special education services and supports. In most instances, resolutions are determined through discussions at IEP meetings or conferences. In rare cases, mediation processes may be initiated as prescribed in IDEA's due process procedures. Due process, a provision of IDEA, includes guidelines for the mediation of conflicts between parents of a student with a disability and the school. Due process "conflicts" typically involve differing views on the supports and specially designed instruction that constitutes a student's free and appropriate public education (also a provision of IDEA). If a resolution is not determined and the disagreement unresolved, the case may escalate through a series of steps involving the local and state education agencies and ultimately requiring resolution in courts. When escalation occurs to this level, the costs to relationships and actual monetary costs can be expensive. IDEA emphasizes the resolution of conflicts with minimum disruption to students' education and the lives of parents, teachers, and administrators.

Barriers to collaboration may cause fear and anxiety. Parents and/or educators may avoid addressing these barriers because of the discomfort or disruption the barriers might cause. It is crucial to focus on the benefits of collaboration to help diminish the impact of these challenges. Developing a shared understanding and aligning philosophies of what constitutes an appropriate education takes time and energy, but the results can positively impact students, teachers, and parents alike (Smiley, Richards, & Taylor, 2019).

Comprehension check

1   What mandates parental involvement in their child with a disability education?
2   What barriers exist in collaborating with parents?
3   What are some ways to overcome these barriers?

References

Brown, N. B., Howerter, C. S., & Morgan, J. J. (2013). Tools and strategies for making co-teaching work. *Intervention in School and Clinic*, 49(2), 84–91.

Caspersen, D. (2014). *Changing the conversation: The 17 principles of conflict resolution*. New York, NY: Penguin Books.

Friend, M., & Cook, L. (2000). *Interactions: Collaboration Skills for School Professionals*. Boston, MA: Pearson.

Girard, K., & Koch, S. J. (1996). *Conflict resolution in the schools: A manual for educators*. San Francisco, CA: Jossey-Bass.

Graziano, K. J., & Navarrete. (2012). Co-teaching in a teacher education classroom: Collaboration, compromise, and creativity. *Issues in Teacher Education*, 21(1), 109–126.

Hanover Research (2012). *The effectiveness of the co-teaching model: Literature review*. Washington D.C.: Hanover Research.

Kaplan, M. (2012). Collaborative team teaching: Challenges and rewards. *Edutopia*. Retrieved from www.edutopia.org/blog/collaborative-team-teaching-challenges-rewards-marisa-kaplan.

Magiera, K., Smith, C., Zigmond, N., & Gebauer, K. (2005). Benefits of co-teaching in secondary mathematics classes. *Teaching Exceptional Children*, 37(3), 20–24.

Mastropieri, M. A., Scruggs, T. E., Graetz, J., Norland, J., Gardizi, W., & McDuffie, K. (2005). Case studies in co-teaching in the content areas: Successes, failures, and challenges. *Intervention in School and Clinic*, 40(5), 260–270.

Moseley, C. (n.d.). Collaboration vs cooperation: What's the difference? Jostle. Retrieved from https://blog.jostle.me/blog/collaboration-vs-cooperation.

Murawski, W. (2019) Successful co-teaching. Council for Exceptional Children: Need to Know. Arlington, VA. Retrieved from www.cec.sped.org/News/Special-Education-Today/Need-to-Know/Need-to-Know-CoTeaching.

Murawski, W. W., & Dieker, L. A. (2004). Tips and strategies for co-teaching at the secondary level. *Teaching exceptional children*, 36(5), 52–59.

National Center for Education Statistics (2019). Children and youth with disabilities. Retrieved from https://nces.ed.gov/programs/coe/indicator_cgg.asp.

Richards, R., Lawless Frank, C., Sableski, M., & Arnold, J. (2016) *Collaboration among professionals, students, families and communities: Effective teaming for student learning*. New York, NY: Routledge.

Smiley, L. R., Richards, S. B., & Taylor, R. L., (2019). *Exceptional students: Preparing teachers for the 21st century* (3rd ed.). New York, NY: McGraw-Hill Education.

Taylor, R. L., Smiley, L. R., & Richards, S. B. (2015). *Exceptional students: Preparing teachers for the 21st century*. Boston, MA: McGraw-Hill.

Welch, M. (2000). Collaboration as a tool for inclusion. In S. E. Wade (Ed.), *Inclusive education: A casebook and readings for prospective and practicing teachers* (pp. 71–96). Mahwah, NJ: Erlbaum.

Witcher, M., & Feng, J. (2010). *Co-teaching vs. solo teaching: Comparative effects on fifth graders' math achievement*. Presentation, Mid-South Educational Research Association Annual Conference, Mobile, Alabama, November 3–4, 2010.

8 Overarching Instructional Concerns

Stephen B. Richards

Objectives: After reading the chapter, students will be able to:

1 Describe executive functioning and the needed skills for students
2 Identify the role of learning strategies in educating students in general education classrooms
3 Describe metacognition and the required skills for students
4 Identify positive and negative student attributions and the role they play in learning
5 Describe pragmatic language use and the impact on social interactions
6 Describe the need for social skills.

While the focus of this text is students with disabilities, this chapter is devoted to topics that affect all students. With the emphasis on achievement testing and academic progress measures, the time for teachers to engage students in knowledge and skill development outside the college and career readiness standards may be diminished. Special education teachers are frequently involved in improving students' executive functioning, learning strategies, metacognition, attributions, pragmatic and social skills, but it is in the general education classroom where these skills need to be applied. The previous chapter discussed collaboration and co-teaching, which are the ideal approach to developing these skills because it benefits all students, not just those with disabilities. Given the diversity of K-12 school classrooms, many students need support in developing these skills to become efficient, effective, and independent learners. The development of these skills begins in elementary grades and continues to prepare students for high school and postsecondary learning. These skills are useful life skills and are needed to be successful in the workplace and community life. Students also begin to develop executive functions from their earliest school experiences. Executive functions, learning strategies, and metacognition are not separate abilities, and interdependently grow and develop across K-12 schooling and into adult life.

Executive Functions

Executive functions comprise several different aspects of a student's abilities from those learned early in school to more complex skills as students progress through school. Developing in early life are skills in paying attention, focusing on and completing a task, controlling inhibitions, flexibility in thinking, and emotional control (National Center for Learning Disabilities, n.d.). Executive functions can be conceived as self-regulatory abilities that enhance school performance and the adjustment to school, home, and the community.

Memory is critical in using executive functions, particularly those involving learning academic content and skills. *Short-term memory* allows students to retain information to hold in the mind temporarily. Information in short-term memory may be limited to "chunks" of information (e.g., phone numbers are chunked into area code, first three digits, followed by last four digits). Information in short-term memory also can decay as even a relatively short period of time passes. *Working memory* is an extension of short-term memory and includes the ability to retain information long enough to use in the immediate situation. For example, a student learning the alphabet must be able to look at a letter and remember what it looks like long enough to copy it down on paper. Working memory is increasingly important over a school career and is an area where some students with learning or intellectual disabilities struggle. Information in short-term memory can be forgotten or retained in *long-term memory*. For example, in a class where students are learning to recite the alphabet without any visual prompting (i.e., seeing the letters), one student realizes they got all the letters correct and in the right order. They continue to practice this recitation until it becomes virtually automatic. Another student recites the alphabet and realizes they also got all the letters correct and in the right order. This student does not practice, and when checked a couple of days later, they have "forgotten" some letters and mixed up the order. The first student used recitation to "get" the alphabet into her *long-term memory* so that she will remember it more or less permanently. The second student thought they had learned the information, but it was stored in their short-term memory rather than long-term memory and therefore the knowledge "decayed" after only a couple of days. There are a variety of opinions as to what and how these three types of memory actually interact as a system (Cowan, 2008). While there are many strategies for acquiring knowledge, saving it, and retrieving it later, strategies rely on the use of all three types of memory, working, short term, and long term.

Being able to attend to a task and persevere until completion is another crucial executive function. In the previous examples, the first student did persevere and practice the alphabet several times until they were sure it was learned and could retrieve it when asked. The second student did not persevere. Nevertheless, the second student can learn perseverance, which will help them acquire alphabetic knowledge. Perseverance should continue to be developed until students (and adults) can bring their mental faculties to bear on problems or tasks and keep working until the task is completed.

Inhibitory and emotional control is necessary to develop perseverance. Students must learn to "ignore" or delay impulses to do other things (play a video game, talk to a peer, check their phone) to maintain attention and complete tasks (University of California–Berkley Center for Teaching and Learning, n.d.). Similarly, students need to control emotional reactions to events and learn to apply reasoning skills. Our second student in the alphabet example at first may have been frustrated when assessed and did not know the information. However, they may have learned the need to practice more often to achieve the mastery that the first student exhibits. The second student can demonstrate emotional control by resisting an impulse to act out, and reason that perseverance and practice is a way to approach and master the task. In that same class, both students are learning to be flexible in their thinking when the language arts class ends and the teacher shifts to math. The students learn to manage that shift without becoming frustrated or having a significant loss of attention. This flexibility demonstrates inhibitory and emotional control.

Over time, students learn more complex executive functions such as setting goals, making and implementing plans to accomplish the goals, monitoring their progress toward achieving the goals, and making adjustments depending on whether the plan is successful or not (National Center for Learning Disabilities, n.d.). These *self-regulation skills* assist students in becoming independent and effective learners in various tasks and content areas. Students also learn to organize their school lives by using a calendar, keeping up with their books and materials, writing down assignments, and managing their time. Organizational skill development is an area in which many students, especially those with disabilities, struggle as they are expected to be more independent learners. These abilities emerge over time and should grow increasingly effective and sophisticated. Students should learn to plan for a school day, complete a 4-week science project, prepare for a social studies test, write an original poem, and prepare for a sports event on Friday night. Memory, self-control, goal setting, organizational skills, and self-regulation are all factors in accomplishing these tasks. Executive functions serve as the foundation of learning and develop into abilities to manage work, home, and community life in adulthood. Learning and improving these skills is dependent on developing learning strategies and metacognitive skills.

Comprehension Check

1 What skills are included in executive functions?
2 What role does memory play in learning?
3 What are self-regulation skills?

Learning Strategies

Learning strategies are the tools of learning. They provide students with options for acquiring, storing, retrieving, and applying knowledge and skills. These skills are applicable across all academic curriculum areas, but some strategies may be more useful than others in any given learning situation. Therefore, students need a variety of learning strategies to be successful. When students are taught an assortment of learning strategies, individual students can discover which approaches work best for them. Some students learn these skills on their own, or they may be coached by a parent, an older sibling, a class peer, or observe how someone else approaches a learning task. Others do not learn these strategies incidentally or through coaching by family or peers, and need direct instruction. Without direct instruction, these students are not equipped to achieve academic progress. Students with disabilities are often among those students who lack any or a sufficient repertoire of learning strategies. These students benefit from direct instruction on how to learn and on a lesson's learning objectives.

Imagine you are teaching a classroom of diverse learners. Some are very high achievers, while others struggle to stay on task, complete assignments, and make the needed progress in the general education curriculum. You give the students a learning objective, "Discuss the importance of World War II in lifting the U.S. out of the Great Depression." You have provided the students with UDL's multiple means of representation. Lessons have included their social studies text, lectures and discussions, historical photos and videos, a guest speaker who lived during the Great Depression and WWII, and study time for answering questions. On Friday, students know they will be taking a quiz on the three means by which WWII helped the U.S. economy and increased employment. Your high achievers "ace" the quiz. Many students score in the B range, some in the C range, and a few score D or F. You notice the ones who scored C or worse tend to be the same students on each quiz. One of those students is open to talking with you about his struggles. You ask him why he did so poorly on the quiz; he says

> "I was in class and listened to everything discussed and everyone's questions. I really liked the guest speaker and the documentary we saw, and I read the chapter in the book about the Great Depression and WWII. I swear, I did. I don't know why I didn't do well on the quiz."

The student is truthful. He and you may not realize that he doesn't know how to listen, view videos, and read a textbook in ways that help him remember what he needs to know and how to prepare for a short answer quiz.

Bloom's Taxonomy

It is important in this discussion to review what is commonly referred to as Bloom's taxonomy. The taxonomy is a hierarchical organization of educational objectives from less to more complex. The emphasis in the taxonomy is on identifying specific learning objectives that clarify for teachers and students alike what is being taught and what students are expected to know and do. Figure 8.1 includes Bloom's taxonomy, as presented by the Vanderbilt University Center for Teaching, retrieved 05/2020.

The taxonomy uses *remembering* as the least complex task and continues through *understanding, applying, analyzing, evaluating,* and *creating* demands. It identifies verbs that are action-oriented, specific, observable, and measurable. When verbs are specific, observable, and measurable they can be used to plan instruction and devise assessments that measure student progress.

The taxonomy is essential for clarity and identifies the variety of learning strategies used for each level. For example, a *remembering* objective states, "Students will recognize the three branches of the U.S. government," which could be assessed through a multiple-choice quiz or an exit slip requiring students to list the three branches. However, a *creating* objective that states, "Students will investigate and present the interactions of the three branches of government," would require a more complex assessment, perhaps using a rubric describing the content, components, and quality of the presentation. The creating objective would take more time for teaching and learning than would the remembering objective. The college and career readiness standards are similarly arranged in part from less to more complex, particularly when viewed

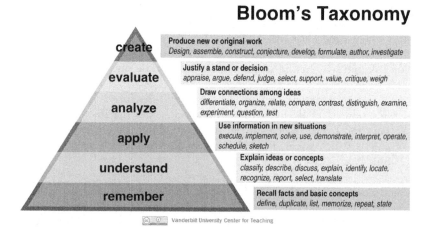

Figure 8.1 Bloom's Taxonomy

across all the K-12 grades in each academic area such as English language arts, mathematics, science, social studies, and so on. Other areas such as art, music, and health/wellness can also rely on a taxonomy of less to more complex knowledge, skills, and application. For example, being able to identify ascending or descending scales in music is less complex than playing the scales on an instrument.

A key to using Bloom's taxonomy is identifying what students must *do* to demonstrate they have acquired the learning objective. In turn, how the students demonstrate their learning is instrumental in selecting and applying useful learning strategies. In the branches of government objectives, the remembering would require students to use a strategy that would allow them to remember and recognize the branches in a multiple-choice quiz. If students must list the three branches, they must remember well enough to recall and list them. The more complex objective is likely to involve many different skills, including remembering information, sorting it, identifying what is most relevant, investigating each branch's role and how the system of checks and balances should work, and so on. Creating the presentation itself also requires more complex skills than taking a quiz or creating a simple list. In turn, in accomplishing the creating objective, students would apply a variety of strategies to meet these more complex demands in learning. The more specific the objective and assessment of learning are, the better guidance it provides students on the appropriate strategies to use. The more complex the learning and assessment, the more students must use their metacognition (discussed later in this chapter) and executive functions.

Various Learning Strategies

There are nearly endless possibilities for strategies for learning. However, some strategies have been used for many years and are "tried and true." As suggested earlier, co-teaching is an excellent model for teaching students learning strategies. During co-teaching, one can teach the academic content while the other demonstrates the necessary learning strategies for acquiring, retrieving, storing, and applying it. Additionally, when strategies instruction is involved, having two teachers in the classroom allows them to focus on smaller groups or even individual students who may need extra help.

The following is a selected list of learning strategies teachers may implement in lessons to assist students (summarized from the University of California–Berkley Center for Teaching and Learning, n.d.):

Think-Pair-Share. In this strategy, students think for themselves about a question or concept presented. They then pair up with a peer to compare thoughts. Finally, each shares their ideas in a larger group, so all benefit from one another's background knowledge, experiences, and perspectives.

Quick Write. In a quick write, students write for a brief period about what they know. This is used to identify their knowledge of a topic, understanding from a reading, or lesson comprehension.

Polling. Software programs allow teachers to construct "quizzes" that can be presented and answered via computer. Each student answers each question, but results are generally shared by group results so that students can check their answers.

Jigsaws. In this approach, the content is divided into sections, and small groups of students are responsible for teaching a section to the whole class. There are as many small groups of students as sections to ensure the entire content is taught. Each group takes notes, writes down the main ideas and important details. The small groups then share their findings with the whole class. Sometimes, as an interim step, each group member is assigned to an "expert" group of all small group members who have a particular section of content. Those experts compare findings, clarify any discrepancies in their understanding, then each expert returns to share their results with their original small group.

Sorting Tasks. Teachers provide separate strips that include a series of statements or actions that must be arranged in the correct order (e.g., who were the last five presidents in order). Small groups or pairs of students work together to get the right sorting (University of California at Berkeley–Center for Teaching and Learning, n.d.).

Several of these strategies generate collaboration and cooperation among students. Polling and Quick Writes are more individually oriented. Both approaches have their uses and place. Collaboration is considered a 21st-century skill necessary in nearly all aspects of life, particularly in school and work. Yet, people must also be able to work independently. While the following strategies may be taught as a group lesson, they are designed for individuals to use to facilitate comprehension, improve writing, and enhance study skills.

Identifying Main Ideas and Details. Identifying the main idea and details is one of the more common learning strategies and is included in the college and career readiness standards. Some students do not know how to "read" a text to comprehend and remember the content. Using graphic organizers and teaching students how to identify critical information will help in comprehension and retention.

Text Features. Text features include bolded terms, subheadings, tables, glossary, chapter outlines, and so forth that organize content in written materials used in schools. Teaching students how to use text features to understand how a chapter or article is organized will help them identify the main idea and details and answer questions.

Draft, Edit, Revise, Edit, Publish. A common strategy for writing projects and assignments is to first draft all thoughts and ideas without regard for correct grammar and punctuation. This draft is then checked for accuracy and edited for grammar and punctuation. It is further revised for clarity and published in the appropriate format. This process provides students with the specific steps necessary to improve their writing. The use of rubrics, peer reviews, and checklists can assist students in meeting these requirements.

Outline and Notetaking. Particularly in classrooms where lectures and discussions are used as a significant strategy for instruction, learning how to outline and take notes is valuable to capturing relevant content. Allowing peer comparisons for additions, deletions, and revisions of outlines or notes helps to ensure the key concepts have been identified and written down. Teaching outlining and notetaking skills and incorporating text features can also be beneficial for independent content reading activities and preparing for quizzes and tests. These strategies can be expanded into creating *graphic organizers, story maps, concept maps, K-W-L charts,* and other means of organizing one's thoughts and learning.

Self-Questioning and Rehearsal. These strategies are similar and commonly used in studying for tests or similar learning tasks. These involve writing out questions on flashcards or study guides (e.g., Who wrote Macbeth? When did the events happen? How did the witches mislead Macbeth while telling the "truth"?). The student answers the questions or flashcards to rehearse the information. These strategies are more beneficial when teachers provide a potential list of questions or other material to demonstrate student learning (Smiley, Richards, & Taylor, 2019).

Case Study 8.1

You are teaching a sixth-grade general education class. It is September and you have been assigned a special education co-teacher. You and your co-teacher have noticed that your students appear to have difficulty in using their social studies text. When you ask questions regarding literal comprehension, many students have difficulty locating the information without prompts. Most students find answering inferential questions nearly impossible.

1   Review a sixth-grade social studies text (or other content area as appropriate) and write a plan to teach students how to effectively interact with their text. (Note: if an actual K-12 text in a content area is not available, use a college textbook instead.)
2   Devise a lesson plan centered on an aspect of the content that also includes instruction on one or more learning strategies.

This list is a partial sampling of the many study and learning skills beneficial for students in learning and demonstrating their knowledge. Learning strategies for performing various math tasks include solving computation and word problems. *Mnemonic* strategies using a sentence to help remember specific knowledge (e.g., Every Good Boy Does Fine stands for E,G,B,D, and F, the notes on the lines in the treble clef in music) and procedural steps (e.g., the steps in conducting an experiment). Every content area taught has its applications of or particular strategies that are useful for students. What is most important is that teachers explicitly instruct students on how to use various strategies, depending on the content and the task to learn, and demonstrate learning. Again, many students do not learn these strategies by trial and error. Or they know strategies useful for particular tasks (e.g., multiple-choice quizzes) but lack effective strategies for other or more complex tasks (e.g., taking an essay test or creating a visual presentation). Once students have acquired a variety of learning strategies, they can use their metacognition and executive functions to govern and evaluate how they learn.

Comprehension Check

1   What is the importance of learning strategies in student performance?
2   How does Bloom's Taxonomy help teachers and students understand learning expectations?
3   What are three examples of learning strategies? Why is possessing a variety of learning strategies necessary for achievement?

Metacognition

Metacognition is sometimes referred to as the ability to think about your own thinking. It is the process students use to plan, implement, monitor, evaluate, and revise their strategy to learn. Metacognitive skills develop alongside learning strategy and executive function development. They allow students to realize whether they are comprehending and absorbing the information. Three types of content-area knowledge and skills, declarative, procedural, and conditional, support metacognition. The following discussion of these types of knowledge is summarized from Smiley, Richards, and Taylor (2019).

Areas of Content Knowledge

Students need three types of content knowledge to be successful learners. *Declarative knowledge* is an understanding of what needs to be learned (Smiley et al., 2019). If teachers develop specific learning objectives, the students, in turn, will have a better understanding of what they are expected to know and do. Specific learning objectives also include how the students' learning will be assessed. Consider two examples of learning objectives for a college course:

1   Following reading Chapter 2, class discussions, homework assign-ments, and group collaboration, students will list in the correct order

the five steps in identifying students with disabilities in K-12 schools, as assessed by a short answer 5-item quiz on Friday.

2   After the next four lessons, students will know how K-12 students are placed in special education with 80% accuracy.

The first example provides information about what will occur instructionally, what students are expected to know, and how they will be assessed. Example 2 may appear to be "okay" at first glance. Here, the teacher may know the instructional activities, what students should "know," and how knowledge will be assessed. However, students only know the general content to be learned (how K-12 students are placed ...) and not much else. There may be confusion about what "are placed in" or how "80% accuracy" will be assessed. Will there be a test? Are there chapters that need to be read? Declarative knowledge arms the student with clear ideas of what is to be learned, how instruction will take place, and how knowledge will be assessed.

Procedural knowledge is a direct outgrowth of declarative knowledge and the use of various learning strategies. Procedural knowledge is how students will go about learning (Smiley et al., 2019). In the first example learning objective above, students can begin to plan how they will learn the five steps, in the correct order, to recall and respond to questions in a quiz.

Students can assume that during the various instructional activities, those five steps will be identified and in the correct order. A student equipped with learning strategies will read, listen for, ask questions, and discuss the five steps with others. They may make flashcards for each of the five steps and practice placing or writing them in the correct order. They may ask themselves what each step includes and how it interacts with the other steps in the process. They may rehearse this a couple of times on Thursday and ask a peer on Friday to help them review. With successful practice Thursday and Friday morning review, they enter class, confident in their knowledge for the quiz.

A second student may assume the five steps in the correct order will be presented in class. This student takes notes and identifies those steps in order. In reading the chapter, they do not specifically look for the five steps. The student attends class, reads the chapter, but does little else to prepare for the quiz. On Friday, the second student takes the quiz with confidence but then is unable to recall all five steps and gets confused about the order once the "pressure" is on. When asked to briefly explain various steps, the student can only give vague answers.

Both students have applied one or more learning strategies, but the first student is much more likely to be successful on the quiz because of the strategies used and how they used them. The first student effectively applied procedural knowledge (and incorporated the two types of knowledge), leading them to success. Student one leaves the quiz smiling;

the other student leaves unsure of their success and worried about their grade. When the second student receives a poor grade, they lament the quiz was too hard and the material challenging to master.

Conditional knowledge is also exemplified in our two student examples. Conditional knowledge is knowing when and why to use procedural knowledge (Smiley et al., 2019). Armed with declarative knowledge of what needs to be learned and procedural knowledge of the plan for learning it, student one devised three strategies to assist. First, they focused on ensuring they had all the necessary content information and declarative knowledge. They then used procedural knowledge to develop a study system of flashcards, writing down the steps, and rehearsing the information. Finally, they reviewed with a peer before the quiz. If the learning objective had been worded as the second example, this student would have to try and discern for themselves what was important to know from the instructional activities and would likely try to remember many less relevant facts and concepts.

Suppose the students learn from the teacher on Tuesday that there will be a test on Friday based on the second objective that includes short-answer questions. Student one would then most likely rehearse and self-question facts and concepts that the teacher does not include in the quiz. This student may enter the text on Friday with considerable anxiety as to how they will perform. If they score well, they may tell themselves that their study habits worked. They may note how the quiz was constructed to prepare for future assessments. This student learned something about how the teacher delivers instruction and how to identify important content to use in the future. While the quiz score may not have been as high as they hoped, they are still confident in their ability and procedural knowledge for studying for the next quiz.

The second student lacked sufficient content, procedural, and conditional knowledge and is unprepared for the test and, not surprisingly, scores well below the 80% benchmark. This student leaves the test feeling defeated. They may tell themselves that they attended class, read the chapter and class notes, and still scored poorly on the quiz. This student may worry that they will not do well in the remainder of the course and question whether they are in the right major. They may try to avoid this teacher for future college courses. They may also question whether it is worth studying for future tests since they do not know what "the teacher wants" or how to figure it out.

The two students have similar intelligence levels, comparable home environments, and adequate reading and writing skills. Their success or lack thereof is dependent on using executive functions and metacognitive skills. Over time, in this course and maybe in other classes, their success is affected by their attributions (Smiley et al., 2019). When the three types of knowledge come together for students, they develop beliefs that they can learn and overcome obstacles such as the type of assessment, vague learning objectives, and instructional activities with little variety (e.g., read the text and lecture course). Without declarative, procedural, and conditional knowledge, students may believe school is a place of anxiety where their deficiencies are on display, a place where they are reminded of their shortcomings regularly, and perhaps a place to be avoided altogether. These students may give up, feel anger toward school and the teachers, or be confused and feel inadequate as students.

Comprehension Check

1   Describe metacognition?
2   What is declarative, procedural, and conditional knowledge?
3   How does metacognition intersect with learning strategies to promote student learning?

Attributions

As the term suggests, attributions are related to what you attribute your "success" or "failure" to (the term failure will be used to indicate a lack of adequate success). There are positive attributions (i.e., the student attributes success or failure to their own efforts) and negative attributions (i.e., the student does not attribute success or failure to their own efforts or believes they are not capable as learners). Smiley et al. (2019) noted that students' attributions could often be traced to their use of executive functions, learning strategies, and metacognition. Students who are well equipped in these abilities tend to have positive attributions. In contrast, students who don't have adequate executive functions, learning strategies, and metacognition are at higher risk for negative attributions.

Consider two students who are taking a midterm history exam. One student brought to bear abilities to focus attention, develop a study plan, use strategies they know are helpful to them, and monitors whether their efforts are resulting in successful exam preparation. The other student was not adequately equipped with these same skills. This student peruses the text chapters covered by the exam the night before while listening to music and texting a couple of friends. They read the class notes the morning of the exam while eating breakfast and conversing with friends about the weekend activities.

The first student scores an A on their exam and attributes the achievement to their efforts. They were focused, planned, studied, and reviewed using various strategies while adjusting the study plan to ensure they learned everything the exam might cover. Student one has a positive attribution and believes their grade was a direct result of their own effort.

The second student scores a D on the exam. They attribute the lack of achievement to "not being very good at history." After all, they "read" the text the night before and "read" class notes the morning of the exam.

This student may think they were just "unlucky" in the items the teacher included on the history exam or that the history professor is "just too hard." They have negative attributions in two respects. First, this student attributes their poor performance to an innate inability (not being very good at history) rather than their study plan and execution. This belief in an inherent inability is perhaps the more negative attribution, which may lead to the conclusion that they are incapable of learning certain content areas because they "just don't get it." In turn, this student may give up in those content areas or even give up on school in general. The second negative attribution is related to being "unlucky" based on what the teacher included in the exam or that the professor is "just too hard." Being unlucky suggests poor performance is outside their realm of control and the belief the professor is too hard reinforces the notion that their poor exam performance was caused by the teacher and rather than their own efforts. This type of negative attribution can be quite challenging to overcome if the student blames the teacher for their performance (e.g., "They are an awful teacher and they hate me."). In either attribution, the student believes they have lost control of how they will perform in school.

Repeated success can encourage positive attributions, while repeated failure can promote negative attributions. However, students can have positive or negative attributions when they experience failure. Imagine that both students are also taking a science exam.

The first student is overconfident in their knowledge of science and decides to only do a check of class notes the night before the exam, and focuses their efforts on the history exam. The second student relies on their usual study plans of perusing the text the night before and reading the notes before the exam. However, while studying for the science exam, they do not listen to music or text anyone while perusing the science text. The first student has consciously decided to spend most of their efforts on the history exam. The second student follows the preparation plan they know and use for all subjects and reads the text and class notes.

Student one received a C– on the exam. Their first reaction is, "I didn't study enough. I won't do that again when the final exam comes along. I'll be sure to prepare more thoroughly for that one." This student knows to adjust their overall exam preparation efforts to give them sufficient time to study well for both the history and science final exams. The attributions are still positive despite the disappointing performance. This student acknowledges their efforts are what determined the poor performance.

The second student scores a B on the science exam and is pleased with the grade. The student may have a negative attribution though if they think "the teacher is nice; she knows how to teach; she likes me more than other teachers." Or the student thinks, "Wow, I got lucky because that exam was easy." With both types of thoughts, the student is still not

	Student Succeeds	Student "Fails"
Student controls academic performance. Belief in self as a learner.		
Positive Attributions	I studied hard. I made plans and they worked.	I didn't study enough. I will plan better next quiz.
The student loses faith in own abilities. Others control academic performance.		
Negative Attributions	I sure was lucky on that quiz. The teacher must really like me.	I just can't learn this stuff. The teacher hates me.

Figure 8.2 Positive and Negative Attributions

attributing success to their efforts and believes the teacher and luck control how well they do. They do not consider how study skills and a distraction-free environment impacted their degree of success. Figure 8.2 depicts how positive and negative attributions might be expressed.

Attribution Retraining

Smiley et al. (2019) point out that when teachers focus on student attributions, positive ones can be developed, and negative ones reduced. First, teachers must teach content along with how to develop and apply executive functions, learning strategies, and metacognitive skills. Co-teaching is a valuable model for accomplishing this. Second, teachers encourage students to recognize and believe that they are in control of their performance in school. Third, teachers assign tasks that direct students in using their abilities to achieve success. It may begin with lower-level tasks in Bloom's Taxonomy (*remembering* and *understanding*) and eventually move toward higher-level learning (*applying, analyzing, evaluating,* and *creating*).

Case Study 8.2

You are a general education teacher in a tenth-grade general education class. You have three students with IEPs for specific learning disabilities among your 24 total students. You have noticed that two of these three IEP students are always making remarks such as "This is too hard to do." "I can't do this by myself." "I don't know why I even have to learn this stuff – I don't care about learning this stuff." "Why are teachers always making me do things that I can't do; you all must hate me."

1 What types of attributions are these students displaying?
2 What is likely the cause of these attributions?
3 What steps could you and your special education co-teacher take to try to "reverse" these attributions?

If nothing else, teachers should be sensitive to student statements that indicate negative attributions (e.g., "I'm stupid; I just can't learn this stuff; that teacher doesn't like me and is trying to make me fail."). Middle and high school teachers should be especially sensitive to attributional statements. By the upper grade levels, students may have experienced enough difficulties/failure that they are losing faith and hope in achieving academic success. Teachers should respond to these negative comments by talking to the student, helping them develop learning strategies, providing opportunities for success by using those strategies, and encouraging them to believe in their own abilities (Smiley et al. 2019).

Comprehension Check

1 Define attributions.
2 Provide examples of positive and negative attributions.
3 What might be the long-term effects of negative attributions?

Social Skills

One important reason we all attend school is to develop socially. We learn many skills about how to interact with adults and peers. Isolation or exclusion from the social interactions of school can be hurtful to any student if they are also not afforded opportunities through out-of-school interactions with peers. Students with disabilities may promote their own exclusion via their use of language. Bear in mind, speech disorders and language disorders are not the same thing as we have discussed previously. Language disorders do not necessarily affect a student's ability to produce perfectly intelligible speech in terms of sounds, words, and phrases. Instead, students with specific learning disabilities, emotional or behavioral disorders, and intellectual disabilities may display language disorders that are secondary to their primary disability. Language disorders, which affect how well a person processes and uses language, can have a serious impact on communication skills.

Students attend school to develop socially and learn how to interact with adults and peers. Social skills are verbal and nonverbal skills (speech, gestures, facial expressions, conversation skills) people use daily to communicate with others. These skills are typically learned through modeling or watching others successfully navigate social situations, through adult prompting/teaching, and trial and error. At times though, people struggle to learn these skills through modeling alone, they may not absorb prompts well, and they may make the same errors repeatedly. This failure to learn social skills is especially applicable, but not limited to students with disabilities. Failure to learn these skills can have harmful consequences to a student, including isolation or exclusion from social interactions. One area of particular concern regarding language use and social success is pragmatics.

Pragmatics

Pragmatics is how language is used to communicate and involves a variety of skills (Smiley et al., 2019). This discussion will focus on two pragmatic skills that affect students socially. The first is the ability to initiate, maintain, and end conversations; in simple terms, carry on the turn-taking or the give and take of a conversation. Second is the ability to read the unspoken communication signals that people send; in simple terms, the ability to recognize and comprehend nonverbal cues from others.

When a person is deficient in these two pragmatic skills, they are likely to have some difficulty interacting with adults and establishing and maintaining peer relationships. Conversational skills are a necessity for students to enjoy satisfying social interactions. If a student does not know how to approach other students to begin or join a conversation, they are likely to avoid such situations and repeatedly derail their own social efforts. Students who are poor at asking and answering questions, interrupt conversations, go off-topic, or do not know how or when to end a conversation will have greater difficulty making friends. It may also affect the quality of their interactions with teachers and other adults in the school. If these deficiencies are coupled with a diminished ability to read body language and facial expressions, there is real potential for a student to experience social isolation or exclusion. The social issues a student may face can be more hurtful than any academic deficiencies. For example, a student who barges into a conversation uninvited, and perhaps off-topic, may very well "put off" those peers from whom they seek recognition. This rejection from peers can cause more psychological pain than struggles in reading or math.

Similarly, if a student only answers questions with a single word, conversations may be superficial to others and short in length. If a student does not know how to ask appropriate on-topic questions, then a conversation is likely to end quickly. Students who do not comprehend when another person signals it is time to end a conversation and instead press on with statements or questions may be perceived as a nuisance. When a student does not adjust their conversation to match their communication partner (for instance, a peer-to-peer conversation vs. a

student-to-teacher interaction), they may severely impact their own interactions with adults and peers. For example, a student who speaks to their
teacher as if they are talking to peers in their neighborhood may use
language or bring up topics inappropriate for school and even offensive
to teachers.

Teachers often rely on nonverbal signals (e.g., "the stare," moving
toward a student, holding up a hand to signal "stop," holding up the
index finger to signal wait) to correct inappropriate behavior and promote classroom management. A child who ignores or does not understand these signals may be in trouble more often and seen as a behavior
problem, which may cause the student to exhibit more inappropriate
behavior (e.g., not knowing when to stop what they are doing).

Pragmatics can be a tremendous challenge for some students and perhaps their most significant barrier to enjoying social connections and
healthy relationships with teachers and peers. These students need direct
instruction with guided practice to learn conversational skills and understand the subtle nonverbal signals sent by others. These students may not
learn these skills through modeling and observing others using those
skills. They may also be less aware of how others perceive them socially
(e.g., as a friend, as an acquaintance, or as someone with whom to maintain minimum contact). Nearly everyone would agree that not having
friends in school is a significant deficit that may seriously impact a student's adjustment to and attitude toward school. These deficits can continue throughout life, impacting adulthood as well. As teachers, we have
known students whose interactions were largely with family members
because they had no or very few friends. We have had to teach a high
school student how to ask a date to go to the prom. Similarly, we have
been involved in communication training of students in workplaces to
know how to interact with customers, co-workers, and their supervisors.
People don't typically suffer social isolation and exclusion as a result of
having fewer academic skills. They do suffer social isolation due to a lack
of social skills.

Teachers can use direct instruction, particularly in co-teaching situations, to take advantage of teachable moments when social interactions
go awry. They can promote acceptance and encourage peer interactions
through collaborative projects and activities. While academics should
always be a key component, some may argue that the inclusion of students with disabilities (particularly those with more moderate/severe disabilities) is as much to promote social acceptance among nondisabled
peers as it is about academic skill acquisition. Indeed, over my lifetime, I
have noted that younger generations tend to be more accepting of human
differences than when I attended K-12 schools in the 1960s and 1970s. In
those times, isolation was often enforced in schooling by excluding students with disabilities altogether or relegating them to special schools or
classrooms to minimize interactions with nondisabled peers. These

practices may have had the intention of "protecting" the students with disabilities, but everyone must take some risks to find success and happiness in school and life, understanding there will be some rough spots. We owe this to students with disabilities. It is our obligation as educators to try to minimize the risks and rough spots and encourage and celebrate friendship and acceptance of others who are different from ourselves.

Comprehension Check

1   What are pragmatic skills?
2   How do pragmatic skills affect social interactions?
3   How can students with and without disabilities benefit from social interactions?

References

Bloom's Taxonomy (n.d.), Vanderbilt University Center for Teaching, retrieved 05/2020.

Cowan, N. (2008). What are the differences between long-term, short-term, and working memory? Retrieved from www.ncbi.nim.nih.gov, 06/2020.

National Center for Learning Disabilities. (n.d.) What is executive function? Retrieved from www.ldonline, 05/2020.

Smiley, L. R., Richards, S. B., & Taylor, R. L. (2019). *Exceptional students: Preparing teachers for the 21st century*. Columbus, OH: McGraw-Hill.

University of California at Berkeley Center for Teaching and Learning (n.d.). Active Learning Strategies. Retrieved from teaching.berkeley.edu, 05/2020. What is executive function? Retrieved from www.understood.org, 06/2020.

Index

Locators in **bold** refer to tables and those in *italics* to figures.

Made in United States
Orlando, FL
03 March 2022

15360753R00096